An Elephant Ate My Arm

"Delightful and insightful travel tales that combine a love of nature with **astute observations about the human condition**. Bonus: Provocative discussion questions make this a **perfect read for book clubs!**"

— Judith Horstman, Author, *The Scientific American Healthy Aging Brain*

Halfway through *An Elephant Ate My Arm,* King describes her own method: "I had a nose for weirdness." Indeed, King finds **weirdness and wonderfulness** all over the world, and she describes both with **verve and humor.** But something else is at play here: a **willingness to explore** not just the outer world, but the inner one, too. To this personal journey she brings understated grace.

—Constance Hale, Journalist, travel writer, and author of *Sin and Syntax*

"Hilarious, informative, sometimes profound—King once again delivers for adventuresome readers and travelers.

— Linda Watanabe McFerrin, Author of *Navigating the Divide* and *The Hand of Buddha*

"King is **relentlessly inquisitive**, and her curiosity propels her to the far corners of the globe seeking answers. 'How do eagles have sex in the sky?' is just one of the questions that lead to revelatory discoveries in *An Elephant Ate My Arm.*"

— Michael Shapiro, Freelance writer for National Geographic and author of *The Creative Spark*

"What a **delightful excursion to magical places** and once-in-a-lifetime experiences! Each chapter of *An Elephant Ate My Arm* will spur you on to hit the road and discover the wonders and life lessons of travel. From the beauty of the butterfly's eye in Costa Rica to the witch in a bottle in England, King **combines astute observations with a keen writer's pen.** If you yearn to discover the unusual as you wander the world, this book is a must-read."

— Pamela Burke, Journalist and founder of *The Women's Eye* website and podcasts

"King blends a vast amount of knowledge and perceptions with her own special **quirky insights** and descriptions. Her science background and **philosophical curiosity** offer you delectably deep insights combined with chuckles and belly laughs. As you finish each story, it's hard not to reach for the temptation offered in the next totally unique experience."

— Diane LeBow, Ph.D., President emerita, Bay Area Travel Writers

"The Bald Eagles of Klamath Basin have been called the greatest gathering of eagles outside of Alaska. And King has done the hard work for you—rousing before dawn, wearing five layers of insulation to fend off the icy air, repeatedly wiping the fog off her binoculars. And then there they are—massive dark-bodied eagles flying out of a shallow canyon. The best thing about King's essays is that you already know Laurie. She is your pal, your sister, **your shadow-person who does the adventure with you and says just the thing you wish you'd said."**

—Allen Fish, Director, Golden Gate Raptor Observatory

"King gives us **fascinating stories** of her quirky or behind-the-scenes adventures. Some destinations are places thousands have gone, but King foregoes the guided tours and **learns from the locals** in the shops, staff in the museums, and scientists in the field. I particularly enjoyed getting a closer view of her playful relationship with husband when they travel together, and the introspective moments when she examines the lessons and messages she received from her parents in earlier times. Once again, **I was left wanting more!**"

— Susan Alcorn, Author of *Walk, Hike, Saunter: Seasoned Women Share Tales and Trails*

"The design is fabulous, the titles **delightful and intriguing**, and the STORIES! —a perfect literary vessel for King's insatiable curiosity as she pokes around the globe, delving into exotic locales most travelers never journey to. She **delivers cultural details with panache and a funny bone on the side**."

—Lisa Alpine, Author, *Wild Life, Exotic Life,* and *Dance Life*

"This delightful new volume, An Elephant Ate My Arm, covers the globe with King's **adventures, misadventures and humor.** In the first piece, we encounter a "living" pizza in Kyoto, and in the signature story, a lovable 350-pound baby elephant in Zimbabwe. We subsequently meet among others, goddesses in Malta; artists in Cuba; a man-eating lake in Trinidad; and end up with prophetic butterflies in Costa Rica. These are trips you can take from your armchair if you jump on King's magic carpet and let her take you in her **irresistible style."**

—Joanna Biggar, Author of *That Paris Year* and *Melanie's Song*

"*An Elephant Ate My Arm* makes you a travel companion, fellow food taster and research colleague as King traipses through Alaska, Cuba, Japan, Libya, Russia, Trinidad and beyond. Her style is **gently humorous and extremely readable**; being along for the ride is a delight."

— Jules Older, Multi-award-winning writer whose most recent travel ebook is *Death by Tartar Sauce*

With X-ray vision, King perceives the **real treasure everywhere** she sets foot, whether in Zimbabwe with a baby elephant (who swallows half her arm), pondering shrunken heads in Oxford, England, getting acquainted with the Fat Ladies of Malta, or in an antique mechanical museum in San Francisco. Her **stories excite** the armchair traveler as much as the adventure enthusiast.

—Camille Cusumano, Author of
Tango, an Argentine Love Story

"Dive head first into these tales and you'll not just learn about Malta's "fat ladies," chase New Zealand's tuatara lizards, you'll also revel in the funny and poignant way King takes us along on her meanderings to places far flung. These stories remind me of what I miss most about travel— **connecting more deeply to people and places, local food and wildlife.** If you're as eager to reengage with the world as I am, *An Elephant Ate My Arm* is almost as good as a plane ticket. Almost!"

— Kimberley Lovato, Travel journalist and
author of *Quartraits: Portrait of a Community in Quarantine*
www.kimberleylovato.com

King writes, '**Octopus pancakes seemed unnecessarily adventuresome**. Maybe we should start off with chicken.' For me, 'unnecessarily adventuresome' sums up the book, and why you might want to read it. King's concise and thoughtful stories pull me in and give me the flavor of the place without—for example—the actual octopus pancakes getting anywhere near my mouth. Whereas many of us **less-adventurous travelers might turn away,** she does what we hope she will do, just like we hope the damsel in distress will go into the haunted house (and we really want to know what's in there).

—Bradley Charbonneau, Author of the *Repossible* series

AN ELEPHANT ATE MY ARM

More True Stories from a Curious Traveler

AN ELEPHANT ATE MY ARM

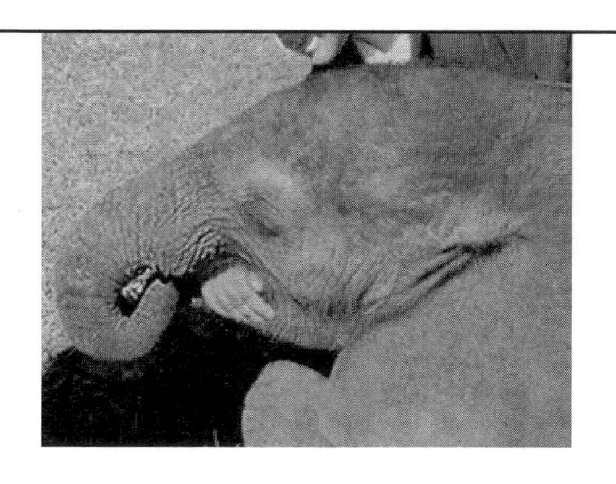

Laurie McAndish King

Destination Insights

In the interest of privacy, I changed the names and identifying details of some of the people I met or traveled with.

Photos:

- Page 38 Flickr by Naparazzi/Wikimedia Commons
- Page 48 is a photo of a photograph that was on display at the Asa Wright Nature Center
- Page 70 and cover © James E. King
- Page 130 courtesy of La Locanda della Querica Calante, Umbria, Italy
- Page 226 Stuart Wolfe, sculpture (bronze), Wikimedia Commons
- Pages xviii, 60, 66, 116, 127, 152, 164, 166, 212, 216-17, 236, 241 © JM Shubin
- Pages 12, 24, 84, 94, 104, 128, 142, 144, 149, 172, 188, 191, 194, 200, 207 © Laurie McAndish King

Diagram on page 124 courtesy of JM Shubin

Published by Destination Insights
www.destinationinsights.com

Cover design, interior design by JM Shubin,
Book Alchemist (www.bookalchemist.net)

CATALOGING IN PUBLICATION DATA:
An Elephant Ate My Arm: More true stories from a curious traveler by Laurie McAndish King

ISBN: 978-1-7348251-9-0 Paperback
ISBN: 978-1-7359954-2-7 eBook

Travel is more than the seeing of sights;
it is a change that goes on, deep and permanent,
in the ideas of living.

—Miriam Beard

Contents

EYES, WINGS AND TONGUES

BODY WORKS

TRANSFORMATION

The Year of Rabbit Holes

Welcome, curious travelers, to twenty-one intriguing destinations: a man-eating lake, the forest home of a three-eyed cannibal, a Caribbean village made of mosaics, an elephant orphanage, the world's first labyrinth, the resting place for a witch in a bottle, a tropical butterfly farm, the perfect site for watching eagle sex…

I wrote most of this book in 2020, the first year of Covid-19. And because travel in the Time of Covid was pretty much out of the question, I took the opportunity to revisit previous journeys—and to think more deeply about those experiences. The alchemy of time and distance infused these stories with a fresh perspective, a new way of understanding, and maybe even a glimmer of wisdom.

Covid provided a powerful lens: the specter of mortality. Every day was tinged with the realization death might be just around the corner. Of course death always *is* just around the corner, especially when we measure our lives in the "long now" of the universe (more on that in the story "Portal to the Uncanny Valley"), but in 2020 the sense of mortality was particularly acute. And, just like in those exercises where you imagine your own funeral or write your own obituary, the result is a closer examination of one's values and beliefs. The experiences I write about in "The Call of the Nightjar" and "Tears and Tiramisu" were particularly challenging in that respect, and are still at work somewhere deep in my psyche.

The flip side of the mortality coin is the joy of appreciating connection, beauty, and being in the present moment—celebrated in stories like "Okonomiyaki," in which Japanese pizza reminds me why I love my husband, and "My Little Red Coquette," in which I experience the magic of sitting still. And sometimes expanding one's awareness to include context is crucial, as I learned while wandering in Moscow's Park of Fallen Heroes and as a dogged voyeur in Libya.

Interior destinations, of course, are the most fascinating of all. Whether you're out trekking, temporarily sheltering in place or planning never to leave the couch again, these stories will bring you to strange, beguiling, disorienting, and thought-provoking places. Follow them to my own favorite neighborhood—the depths of a twisting rabbit hole—

to consider the warren of questions they raise about free will, domestication, crossing the line, compressing time, extinction, *memento mori*, and even rewriting history, when circumstances call for a change in context. They'll bring you the very best of travel: steeping in the terroir of new places, connecting with people different from ourselves, and expanding our well of understanding.

—Laurie McAndish King

The Flavors of Love

ken

Okonomiyaki As You Like It

Japanese pizza reminds me why I love my husband

This pizza is alive, I realize, staring at it in shock. *And it's waving at me.*

I'm going to eat it anyway.

Hungry, tired, and a little cranky after a long day in a country where we don't speak the language, my husband, Jim, and I are in a tiny restaurant in Kyoto. Its specialty is *okonomiyaki*, or "Japanese pizza." Five small tables crowd together, and two other couples, both Japanese, eat in silence.

Jim's stomach rumbles. In front of us sits the pizza, steaming and sizzling on a small grill that's built into the tabletop. Chunks of shredded cabbage and other mysterious lumps jut out of the pizza's lightly browned surface, and there's no tomato sauce in sight. The aroma is hard to identify: Fried fish? Bacon and eggs? Pancakes?

Sprinkled on top of the pizza are thumbnail-sized semi-transparent shreds that look like flakes of skin. They stand as erect as arm-hairs on a winter day, swaying as if alive, waving at me from their plum-sauce pool, then melting and disappearing into the red jam like silent ghosts.

I am about to taste my first bite of okonomiyaki. Although this "Japanese soul food" is served throughout the country, it doesn't really look like something I want to put in my mouth. We are trying it at the suggestion of our hotel concierge.

"Where do local people go for lunch?" we had asked.

"Kiyamachi Japanese pizza. *Hai*," he replied. "Tasty and filling."

"Is it nearby?"

"*Hai*, nearby."

"How do we get there?"

"Between Kiyamachi Dori and Kawaramachi Sanjo," he directed. "Easy to find near kimono store."

Kiyamachi is a historic district known for restaurants, cherry blossoms and nightlife. Wood-fronted shops crowd along each side of a narrow, tree-lined river, and a graceful clump of bamboo or a small maple tree grows near each front door. At night, under an umbrella of stars, paper lanterns glow and the river sparkles with reflected light. We looked forward to a romantic walk to the restaurant.

And so we set out. But soon, two women dressed in green surgical scrubs with matching baseball caps approached, intruding on our intimate stroll. Each wore white gloves and a blue backpack, and carried a long grey tube in one hand. In the other hand each held a big white plastic bag, bulging with unseen contents. As the women came closer, a low roar interrupted the peaceful evening.

"They seem to be wearing vacuum cleaners on their backs," Jim observed.

"You're right—they're actually *vacuuming* the streets."

"How often do you think they empty the bags?"

I didn't want to get into a conversation about housekeeping with him. These Japanese women were cleaning their streets much more meticulously than I had ever cleaned a carpet. Occasionally they pounced on a small piece of trash—a discarded straw or scrap of paper—and dropped it into their plastic bags. I ignored Jim's comment and suggested we move on.

After a little wandering we came upon a tiny restaurant next door to a used kimono shop—this had to be our spot! The storefront itself was barely ten feet wide, its tall window crowded with display plates of bright plastic food, bottles of sake and plum wine, and a big blue poster for Asahi Super Dry beer.

A Shih Tzu puppy with silky white fur poked its nose out the front door. Its ears were two-toned—rusty red and dark brown—and sported mismatched plastic barrettes: pink on its left ear, blue on the right.

I turned to Jim. "Do you think we should eat at a restaurant where the first thing we see is a dog?"

"Don't worry; they don't eat dogs in Japan."

"That isn't what I meant. What if it isn't *clean*?"

"The dog?"

"No. The restaurant."

"You're concerned about the cleanliness of Japanese restaurants?"

He was right—why worry? Everywhere we went this country seemed meticulously clean, and we had just seen two of the reasons—the human street sweepers.

As I pondered our choice of restaurant, an American businessman appeared at the door. He wore an expensive suit and had apparently just finished dinner. A small spot of food adorned his red tie. I guess we still looked undecided because he addressed us.

"You like okonomiyaki?"

"Japanese pizza? We don't know yet."

"You'll like it. It's actually more like a pancake than a pizza. '*Yaki*' translates to *grilled* and '*okonomi*' means *as you like*, because you can order this dish with fish, pork, anything you like. Unless you're gluten-free.

You're not gluten-free, are you?" He brushed an invisible flake of food off his jacket.

"No."

"It's made with wheat flour, starting back during World War II, when rice was in short supply. They fed it to the kids as a snack. The octopus okonomiyaki is a specialty around here."

"Is that what you recommend?"

"Only if you like octopus. I love it; get it every time I'm in town."

Octopus pancakes seemed unnecessarily adventuresome. *Maybe we should start off with chicken*, I thought as we entered the restaurant.

Inside, the elderly couple who ran the restaurant presided over a handful of small tables. Lean and rosy-cheeked, the male proprietor had a high forehead and perpetually raised eyebrows that looked like the wings of an elegant gray bird in flight. He wore a bright purple button-down shirt. The proprietress had a wide smile and an unusual, three-toned hair color: rusty red on top, dark brown at the roots, and white at the temples—almost the exact same three colors as the puppy's coat, minus the barrettes, of course.

We sat at a small table with a rectangular iron griddle inset at the center. The Mrs. brought each of us a steaming white washcloth on a wooden tray, bowing as she placed them on the table. I wiped my hands, enjoying the moist heat and light scent, happy to be participating in a beautiful, time-honored tradition. Jim wiped his face.

"You can't wipe your face with that!" I whisper-hissed, upset at what was certainly a serious faux pas.

He looked bewildered. "I just did. And you don't need to whisper. They don't understand a thing we say."

Jim was right. The couple spoke no English, and we spoke no Japanese. It was going to be an evening of bowing and pantomime. Jim gestured toward the small hibachi grill in the center of our table. "It's just like Benihana's! There's a griddle in the middle. Hey, I made a poem. *Haaaaai-yah!*" He chopped at the air with his hands—his best imitation of a Benihana chef. The lady scurried over to our table, interpreting Jim's raised voice and odd chopping gesture as a request for service. I flushed with embarrassment.

"*Yōkoso. Konbanwa. Nanika otetsudai shimashou ka?*" she asked, bowing slightly.

We stared dumbly at her for a moment. Then I tried for any English she might understand. "Hello. Good afternoon. Good evening."

"*Nanika o nomimono wa ikagadesu ka?*"

"*Hai?* Yes?"

"*Menyū ga sukidesu ka?*"

"*Hai.*" Clueless, I shrugged my shoulders.

When it became clear we couldn't order from a menu written in Japanese, the proprietress shuffled us out to the front window of the restaurant, where we could point to plastic representations of the food we wanted. But what *did* we want? I couldn't remember the word *okonomiyaki*, let alone pronounce it. "What do you think?" I asked Jim, eying the shiny plastic food. "That huge plate of cooked green leaves might be tasty."

"It's undoubtedly delicious," he agreed. "But not very Japanese-looking. We need something we can't get at home."

"That bowl of noodles looks Japanese."

"It's probably very tasty, but it looks like a bowl of juicy worms! *I'm* not eating that."

Then we saw the okonomiyaki, a pancake dolled up with a topping of dark plum sauce, squeeze-bottle zigzags of mayonnaise, and a scattering of chopped scallions. This was the dish we had come for. We pointed, smiled, and said, "*Hai!* Yes!"

The lady understood. She led us back inside where we sat at the table with a built-in propane-heated grill. She pointed at the grill, then put her palm near it and shook her head. We got the message: The grill is hot; don't touch!

Then she pantomimed that we would prepare the

pancake ourselves. We had already successfully ordered a couple of Asahi Super Dry beers, but I wasn't optimistic about the rest of the evening. Which ingredients should we request—and how would we communicate our choices?

The beer had further dampened Jim's inhibitions—not that he had many to begin with—so he did the practical thing: tucked his hands into his armpits, waved his elbows up and down, and squawked like a chicken. *Baaaawck. Bawck-bawck-bawck.* It must have seemed like a safe bet; chicken sounds are pretty much the same in any language. But it didn't look safe. Jim is a big guy, and we were in a tiny space. I worried that his flapping elbows would crash into the woman at the next table.

Jim continued ordering. He put a finger to the front of his nose and pushed it upwards, adding a couple of *squeee*-like sound effects.

I felt—and not for the first time—as though I were dining with a twelve-year-old boy. Surely the owners would kick us out at any moment. "So we're getting the chicken and pork then?"

"Yes," Jim replied with a wink, "unless you want to figure out how to order the octopus. I don't have enough appendages for a request like that."

The proprietress covered her mouth with one hand and tittered, then bowed and hurried off. Maybe she *did* speak English after all. She returned a few minutes later with large stainless-steel bowls filled with batter, shredded cabbage, chopped chicken, and chopped pork. Success! She motioned for me to add these ingredients to the batter myself. "*Okonomi,*" she said.

"As you like it," I murmured, feeling like a fast learner as I spooned the cabbage and meats into the batter and stirred vigorously.

The woman's eyes widened in alarm. Clearly distressed, she reached out and actually grabbed the bowl from my hands. Time slowed down. I knew I'd done something terribly wrong—but what? And whatever it was, how could it possibly be more of a transgression than Jim's pantomimes?

The Mrs. waited until she had my full attention, then showed us how to gently fold the ingredients in, instead of beating them, and handed the bowl back to me.

"She trusts you now," Jim said encouragingly.

Thus instructed, I ladled batter onto the grill and the pizza sizzled for a few minutes. When it was brown on the bottom, our patient instructor flipped it with a wide spatula and brushed on thick plum sauce while the okonomiyaki finished cooking. When the bottom turned golden brown, she turned off the grill, sprinkled a large pinch of bonito flakes on top, and cut the pancake into six flat wedges, like a pizza.

This is when our food starts to wave at us.

"I know they eat a lot of raw food in Japan," says Jim, "but this thing looks like it's alive, and we have nothing to kill it with." He's right. The eerie little flakes of skin are nodding in the heat, waving *hello* ... and I am going to eat them.

Without a fork or knife, we are forced to eat small bits of the pancake slices with chopsticks—not an easy task, but definitely worth the trouble. Our chicken-and-pork okonomiyaki is delicious: warm and savory, crispy on the outside, soft on the inside, and flavored with creamy mayonnaise, tart plum sauce, and salty bonito flakes.

Jim points to the bonito flakes. "I think these are from a dead body."

This time I don't bother to scold him, finally realizing it really doesn't matter what he says. I also realize I *love* that about him—that, unlike me, he is far more interested in connecting and communicating than in worrying about whether he might look foolish. He's willing to take things in stride, whether it's an obsession with tidy streets, a dog in barrettes, or a pizza with a will of its own. Thanks to Jim, we have discovered a delicious dish—of soul food, no less—just "as we like it." And we've enjoyed an evening with the delightful proprietors of this Japanese restaurant through pantomime, food, and laughter.

My Extra-Virgin Experiment

On the civilizing effects of an ancient elixir

I have a thing for extra virgin olive oil. Some might call it an obsession, but I prefer to think of it as a love affair. I've chased that golden-green elixir around the world, savoring its subtle inflections: grassy, fruity, nutty. My husband has waited patiently in elegant tasting rooms as I sipped varietals and cultivars and single-estate standouts, robust early harvests and pale, buttery award-winners.

At home, extra virgin olive oil is my favorite afternoon snack. I pour it onto a cracker and admire it there in a tiny, shimmering pool—surrounded by a dollop of hummus to keep it from falling off. After all, it's the olive oil I'm after. Its leafy hue reminds me of hot summer afternoons. Its peppery burn lashes mischievously at the back of my tongue. Its light viscosity slides luxuriously down my throat. It moistens my lips and glistens on my chin. I smooth the excess onto my hands and elbows. I'm often tempted to smother every inch of my body with the unctuous condiment. I did that once, and felt like an awesome Greek goddess ... until the fruit flies started circling. It also made my bed sheets smell somewhat rancid—a decidedly ungoddess-like effect.

It's not surprising then, with this obsession, that from the minute I started planning my Greek vacation I knew the exotic liquid would have to play a part in the experience. Olive oil is a crucial part of the Mediterranean diet, which is said to support a long and healthy life. It may be the fresh fruits and vegetables, whole grains, legumes, fish and moderate amounts of red wine that actually produce the desired effect, but I prefer to think it's all about the olive oil. Anti-inflammatory, high in phytonutrients and antioxidants, and said to be helpful in preventing maladies as varied as Alzheimer's disease, breast cancer, high blood pressure, obesity, stroke, and type 2 diabetes, it could probably replace one's primary care physician. It has even been credited with enlarging breasts when applied properly.

In fact, olive oil has played an important part in the human experience for millennia. *Kırkpınar*, or olive oil wrestling, is the world's oldest documented sporting event, dating back at least to 2600 BCE, and is recognized by UNESCO as an Intangible Cultural

Heritage. But, in my opinion, olive oil has played its most significant role in human experience as an ingredient in soap. Without soap, we'd still be licking our own skin to get rid of the dust and dirt of everyday life, which might be good for lingual dexterity, but would have set us far, far behind in terms of making time for innovations and inventions, not to mention government, art and critical thinking. One could even make the argument that soap is the foundation upon which civilization has been built.

According to one legend, soap originated on the island of Lesbos, where animal sacrifice was practiced. The remains of those sacrifices—fat and ashes—flowed from stone altars into the river when rains were heavy. Women washing their clothes in the river noticed how good the laundry looked after their oblations, made the connection between animal fat and cleanliness, and soap was invented. The poet Sappho, one of the first to chronicle the efficacy of soap, is supposedly the namesake of soap making or *saponification.* It being Greece, folks quickly figured out that olive oil was a more convenient ingredient than sacrificial animal fat, and so began the long history of olive oil soap making. And one of the best places to make olive oil soap, I discovered, is on a Greek island.

After a week in Athens—seven days spent slathering

my innards in delicious olive oil—I flew to Crete. From the capital city of Heraklion I hopped a local bus to Knossos, the famed site of spectacular ancient ruins, where I encountered evidence of olive oil's importance in ancient times. There, a prominent grouping of gigantic terracotta amphorae—once containing hundreds of gallons olive oil—huddle together like friends frozen in timeless conversation. Nearby, I came across a fresco of elegant Mycenaean maidens dancing in front of olive trees. As I admired the image, my wizened guide, Charidinos, extolled the virtues of olive oil with irrefutable logic: "*Elia* means *olive tree*, or *tree of wisdom*, in Greek," he explained. "So you see, two or three spoons of olive oil every day will make the mind sharp and the body strong!"

Back in Heraklion I discovered yet another way to enjoy the oil of my dreams. I decided to take a class in olive oil soap making. It would be the perfect finale to my Greek explorations. I was pretty sure I remembered that soap making requires lye, or some other highly caustic chemical, but the instructor, Gregory, was a chemist when he wasn't teaching tourists to make soap, so I figured he'd be well-versed in safety. Besides, I could give the soap as a gift to my son's girlfriend, Debbie, who loves fragrant lotions and skin care products. I hadn't found a gift for her yet, and this would be truly Grecian. It would also be an expression of my affection, since it would demonstrate that I'd taken time—several hours, in fact—from my peregrinations to do something thoughtful for her. I signed up.

I expected the soap-making experience to take place either in a chemistry lab or in a small cottage with an ancient stone altar surrounded by trees and friendly woodland animals. But the taxi delivered me to an apartment in the suburbs. Two young couples joined me for the class; one couple was from Scotland, the other from Germany. Apparently there's a worldwide interest among young people in soap production ... or in extra virgin olive oil ... or maybe in making thoughtful little gifts to bring home from Greek vacations.

Besides being a chemist, Gregory—in his thirties, friendly, with a headful of beautiful black hair—played in a band. Ikea-like furniture and several guitars crowded his living room. He had set up a small worktable in the kitchen, which had acid green walls. They were the color olives would be if they were electrified, and created a vague feeling of danger. The supplies Gregory had laid out added to the ambiance of peril: Each participant was provided with a pair of protective goggles, rubber gloves, a 4-inch square of aluminum foil to measure ingredients onto, a beaker, and a long glass stirring rod. We all shared a scale and digital thermometer.

It looked quite scientific. In fact, it reminded me of chemistry class—not a good memory. Despite being excellent at following directions, I could never get my experiments to come out the proper way. That is to say, even though they were "experiments," there were still expectations. Often my results were not even close to the normal range—so much so that I began to wonder whether a fellow classmate was sneaking into the lab and sabotaging my careful work, perhaps trying to influence the grading curve to his or her advantage. That's the way I prefer to explain my consistently unsatisfactory results. And that's why I never really liked chemistry. I *wanted* to like it. I loved the idea of mixing exotic ingredients, like an alchemist turning lead into gold, or a witch brewing up love potions—but I was clearly not cut out for it.

So when Gregory gave us a quick chemistry lesson, it went completely over my head. It began with something about micellar aggregates of surfactant molecules dispersed in colloid liquids and the packing behavior of single-tail lipids in a bilayer, sequestering the hydrophobic regions ... and it ended with the fact that soap made from pure olive oil is known to be especially mild.

Gregory also gave us a safety lesson. "It's important to measure all the quantities carefully," he explained, "and to follow my directions exactly. If the ingredients are combined in the wrong order or in incorrect amounts or even at the wrong temperatures, you could end up with both heat burns and chemical burns. Or with an explosion that would decimate my kitchen!"

Gregory held up a small square of aluminum foil from a previous soap-making class. It was burned—perhaps *dissolved* would be a better term, for only half of it remained—where a caustic chemical sitting on the foil square had come into contact with water. We all gasped appropriately.

I donned the safety goggles and volunteered to go first. With Gregory supervising, I combined the initial ingredients and stirred them carefully with the glass rod. The solution clouded and bubbled, then cleared as a chemical reaction heated the beaker until it was so hot it nearly melted my latex gloves. While the class waited for it to cool off, Gregory gave us a concise history lesson: The earliest recorded evidence of the production of soap-like substances dates back to around 2800 BCE in ancient Babylon. Liquid soap was not invented, however, until late in the nineteenth century. In 1898, a man named B.J. Johnson developed a mixture derived from palm and olive oils, and introduced Palmolive brand soap.

While Gregory talked, my solution was cooling off and ready for the next step. "Do you want to add color or scent?" he asked, pulling out small bottles of red and blue coloring. I considered the options. This was an important decision. I wanted it to be just right, but wasn't sure what Debbie would like best. *Hmmm*, I thought, *something pretty and feminine, for sure.*

Finally, I chose red, figuring I'd add just one drop to turn the mixture a delicate, rosy hue. I'd create a pretty pink bar that was exceptionally soothing and moisturizing. Several scents were available, too: yummy chocolate or healing lavender. I decided on the chocolate. I'd had a chocolate massage once in Spain, and it was an absolutely luscious experience. Excited about my decision, I could already envision Debbie lathering up with wonderful pink, chocolate-scented bubbles.

I added the color carefully, following Gregory's instructions. But I didn't get pink. It turns out that adding just one teeny, tiny drop of red to an extra-green, extra-virgin olive oil solution immediately turns it an unappealing shade of brown. And adding the chocolate scent made it clump together—suddenly the whole thing went "off" like a curdled brown hollandaise. I attempted to transfer my "soap" into the mold, but the lumpy mess continued to congeal and wouldn't pour. I had to scoop it out with my awkwardly gloved hands and dump it into the rectangular mold, poking it like lumpy mashed potatoes into the corners. That old chemistry-class curse had followed me all the way to Crete! I persevered, doing my best to flatten the top, to make it look like a beautiful little gem that Debbie would be proud to put on her bathroom sink. But in the end, there was no escaping the fact that it was brown and lumpy, and looked very much like a ... well, like a thing that belongs in another place in the bathroom, a thing that should be flushed ... and never seen again.

What will they think when I try to bring it home through Customs? I worried. I would definitely have some explaining to do. Perhaps Gregory could provide me a certificate of authenticity. And what would Debbie think? I couldn't possibly give her a gift that looked like *you know what.*

After seeing my unfortunate creation, the German and Scottish couples decided to keep their soaps pure and free of any added color or scent. Of course, their bars turned out beautifully: silky smooth in texture, pale Palmolive-green colored, and with a naturally fresh, clean scent.

I left feeling discouraged—clearly an incompetent chemist, a total failure at what should have been a simple process. I had nothing for Debbie. And my homeward flight was first thing in the morning.

As I walked back to my hotel I kept an eye out for souvenirs in Heraklion's countless gift shops, which sold tie-dyed clothing, olive-themed ceramics, and soaps—lots of olive oil soaps in bright, clear colors: lavender, peach, strawberry red, sea-mist green. The scents were lovely, too: vanilla, lemon, jasmine. I chose a pretty yellow, honey-scented bar for Debbie. I hope she likes it.

I gave the brown one to my husband.

Cuba: Full of Flavor

Organic by necessity, delicious by design

Pretty much all I knew about Cuba before I went was that it was one of the last bastions of communism and the home of passionate revolutionaries, photogenic old American cars and tasty pork sandwiches. The rest was a mystery.

So I didn't know what to expect when I visited the organic farm and restaurant in Viñales, a lush agricultural area about 100 miles southwest of Havana. Standing at the entrance, I flicked the farm's business card with my thumbnail and considered its claim. The card said, in bold aqua-colored letters, "*El Paraiso*." The Paradise. It was followed by another line in smaller type: "*Una Pasion Natural*." A Natural Passion.

The early December sun was warm on my back as I looked out over long green rows of lettuce, Swiss chard, onion, cabbage, carrots, radishes and peppers poking up from the brown soil at El Paraiso.

"We have thirteen hectares," our guide, Marilyn, said, "and everything we serve is grown here except the fish." Marilyn was tall and slender and wore a bright yellow top that matched her sunny disposition. Even though English was her second language, she spoke it very well—and, like most Cubans, very quickly. I struggled to keep up.

Honey bees buzzed at the red torch ginger and orange marigolds that brightened a winding pathway. In the distance, flat sugarcane fields morphed into clusters of craggy pine-tree-covered hills that looked like slumbering dragons.

"Twenty percent of what we produce is sold to the government and is then distributed—for free—to a small hospital and a primary school," Marilyn continued. "We are biodynamic and organic. We don't use any chemicals."

"How do you deal with the insects?"

"We plant marigolds with the corn," she explained. "Our oregano, onions, and three kinds of basil help, too." We followed the path to a section where lettuce was sprouting. I smelled mint and anise as my bare legs brushed against wayward plants.

"Sticky traps, like these, help too." Marilyn brushed a bunch of leaves aside, revealing index-card-sized pieces of colored paper interspersed with the lettuce. "Tropical insects love yellow; those traps catch fifty percent of the insects. The white and blue sticky traps catch twenty-five percent each.

"We grow banana, plantain, cashews, strawberries, spinach, and celery. Sugar cane is used for rum and guarapo—that's an aphrodisiac." Marilyn mentioned this matter-of-factly. Hmmm. Was guarapo the key to El Paraiso's "natural passion?" I wondered whether it was included with the hospital and school provisions, but Marilyn didn't give me time to ask.

"We get wood from the forest and use a spring pump for irrigation. Kitchen waste goes to compost, and so do ashes from cooking charcoal," she continued, pointing out key aspects of the operation. Marilyn covered a lot of ground, both literally and figuratively. "The rabbits' dung is used for fertilizer: Earthworms process it, and then we combine it with compost. We feed the rabbits sweet potatoes. Honey, coriander, chickens, geese ..." she kept going, but I was ready to sample the cuisine, so I ambled over to a shaded picnic table and grabbed a seat near some of the other visitors.

Where to begin? A sign on the wall recommended the anti-stress drink El Paraiso was famous for, and even provided the recipe:

Cóctel Antiestrés

Jugo de Piña
1 Hojita de Anís
1 Hojita de Menta
1 Hojita de Hierba Buena
1 Hojita de Albahaca
1 Hojita de Caña Santa
Una Pizca del Leche de Coco
Miel
Canela
Ron opcional

Carlos, our server, brought out tall glasses of the frothy beverage, and translated the list of contents: pineapple juice, anise, spearmint, yerba buena, basil, lemongrass, coconut milk, honey and cinnamon. I tried to remember—were any of those potent anti-stress ingredients? The rum, or *ron*, was probably important if one wanted to experience the full anti-stress effect, but my drink didn't taste alcoholic.

The explanation emerged when Carlos returned holding up what looked, from a distance, like a bottle of rum. "This is *Vitamin R*," he explained solemnly. "*R* is for rum. Officially optional, but it helps with the stress."

Ah-ha! Another clue to that natural passion, I thought, as everyone at the table poured liberally from the bottle of Vitamin R.

The published recipe for Cóctel Antiestrés doesn't reveal all of the beverage's ingredients. When I asked whether the drink was dairy-free, Carlos said no, and brought me a slightly less-foamy version. And I tasted nutmeg, which hadn't been disclosed as an ingredient. But I didn't stress out about it—I couldn't, really. After all, I was in Paradise. And the Vitamin R was flowing freely.

Next up was the organic, biodynamic, chemical-free meal. It was served family-style: crispy mounds of hand-sized taro and cassava chips, a fabulous soup, platters of chicken, delicate fish, tender pork, sweet potato, pumpkin, lettuces, crunchy pickled vegetables, and rice with beans. Silence descended on the table as we scooped up one delicious mouthful after another. Aromatic steam rose from the thick yellow soup. It was full of chunks of sweet vegetables, bursting with flavor. I had to have the recipe.

"Carlos, this soup is delicious. Do you think you could get me the recipe?" I asked boldly, perhaps inspired by the Vitamin R.

Moments later Olga Lidia, the chef and a co-founder of the farm, appeared. Olga had chocolate-colored skin, friendly crinkles around her eyes, and a big smile. Her aqua T-shirt sparkled with hundreds of sequins. She wrote for me in a large, loopy script:

Zanahoria, rábano, pepino, habichuela, malonga, calabaza, col, ajo, cebolla, aji, pimiento, comieno, pimienta (al gusto), aceite, bijol

I assumed it was a list of the ingredients for the soup. "That's a lot of vegetables—and you grow them all here?"

"Yes, so many vegetarians came to the restaurant," Olga explained in Spanish as Carlos translated. "I created this recipe especially for them. But the soup is better—*muy rico*," she added with a wink, "if you include beef, pork, or chicken. It's best with all three." Olga's recipe and methodology—translated below—are simple:

Carrot, radish, cucumber, kidney beans, taro, pumpkin, cabbage, garlic, onion, red pepper, bell pepper, cumin, black pepper (to taste), oil, annatto

Cook all together until the flavor is right.
Serve warm.
Enjoy!

Chef Olga Lidia
Founder of the Farm

Cuban food, I had learned, is much more than pork sandwiches. El Paraiso gave me a good perspective on the first half of the country's farm-to-table arrangement: small-scale growing, companion planting and integrated pest management. Now it was time to visit a *paladar*—one of Cuba's privately owned restaurants, which are often in the homes of their owners.

I felt a little guilty, because most local people can't afford to eat in paladars. Unless they're pulling in foreign money from the tourism industry, Cubans eat mainly rice and beans, with occasional chicken or pork for protein. But paladars are the appropriate place for tourists to eat, and I resolved to infuse money into the country by dining at as many as possible.

"You must visit Paladar Los Mercaderes," my fellow traveler Linda insisted after we'd been in Havana a few days. "The staircase leading up to the restaurant is lined with rose petals. And the owner, Yamil, is *very* handsome." Linda smiled conspiratorially, and I began planning my visit immediately.

When I arrived at Paladar Los Mercaderes, the first thing I saw was a white marble staircase with flickering votive candles and—just as Linda had described them—velvety red rose petals sprinkled on every step, drawing me upwards. I half expected to see sexy lingerie and abandoned shoes scattered at the top. Was there "natural passion" at Cuban paladars, as well as at the farms? What if I'd come at the wrong time of day, and caught someone *in flagrante delicto*? This *was* in someone's home, after all.

Yamil stood at the top of the stairs. "Hello, Laurie.

Nice to meet you." Yes, he was handsome, with glossy hair and twinkly eyes. And he was fully clothed.

"Yamil! Good to meet you. Thanks for taking the time to talk with me. I have to ask the obvious question first. The entrance is so romantic. What's the story of all these rose petals?"

"Well, I will tell you," Yamil said, speaking softly as we sat down at a table near the bar. I had to lean forward to hear him over clatter and conversation coming from the kitchen. This turned out to be a habit of Yamil's, and every time he lowered his voice and said, *Well, I will tell you*, I leaned forward and listened intently.

"I said to my wife, 'Why don't we try to make a restaurant where we would like to go?' And we definitely would love to walk up stairs with rose petals and candles welcoming us. So that is why, since we opened five years ago, every single day we have rose petals—not only on the stairs, but also on the toilet—even when people told us we were crazy to spend the money."

"I'm glad you did; you've created a beautiful restaurant." I glanced around the room. Art hung on every wall and chandeliers glowed beneath high ceilings. Red tablecloths and sparkling dinnerware enhanced the romantic feeling. Three giant windows each opened onto their own small balcony with a private table overlooking the street. Live Afro-Cuban music drifted in on a warm breeze. I began to wish I'd brought my own handsome man along.

"And then our dream started, like that." Yamil continued. "This room where we are sitting now, this was our daughter's room. And that was our bedroom. Look at tiles on the floor; you can see where a wall used to be."

I tried to imagine the space as a home, and wondered what the bedrooms might have looked like, but aromas wafting from the kitchen made it impossible to think of anything but food. "What kind of cuisine do you serve?"

"Seafood, pork, chicken. My wife and I are very picky about food. We focus on bringing the best recipes of the countryside to our menu. When the Spanish came to Cuba, they brought African people, who brought spicy food. My wife's favorite is the spicy seafood dish with fish, shrimp, lobster, and octopus."

Salivating, I asked, "What spices do you use?"

"Well, I will tell you," Yamil said. I leaned in closer. "Cumin, curcumin, oregano ... and we use, of course, *very* good garlic. It's not as big as the one I see in some other countries, but the taste is just amazing. We were forced to be organic before that became fashionable. Now people appreciate that when the food is organic, it's more healthy, you know? Our black beans are very creamy. We call them *frijoles negros dormidos*."

"*Dormidos?*" I thought Yamil had said *creamy*, but maybe I misunderstood. I leaned in even closer.

"That would be like *sleeping* black beans, because they are very creamy," he said. "When you look at the black beans, they look like they are sleeping."

Sleeping black beans? Because they are creamy? There was some part of this metaphor—something about the combination of *sleeping* and *creamy*—that was lost in translation.

"They are exquisite!" he continued enthusiastically. "But these black beans are almost impossible to find in the market, so we went to the countryside to find a family farming them. We do the same with lamb; we have an old man who is feeding them in the natural way. They benefit with us, and we are very happy working with them. This is a winning-winning relationship."

Then Yamil lowered his voice again, as if he were about to divulge a secret. "I will tell you. Happy animals walking free—that makes the quality of the meat very different. With our pork, too, it's from just one family in a small little town."

"What's *your* favorite Cuban food?"

"Me? Definitely, I love pork. It is always on the menu of Cuban people. It's especially good when fed with little coconuts—the fruit of the royal palm tree, *palmiche*. Countryside people discovered this by accident: When they had open cages by the royal palm tree, the flavor is just *amazing*."

"You sound so passionate when you talk about food, Yamil...."

"Yes, well we were very happy when Obama opened possibilities for Americans to visit Cuba, but now we are dramatically affected by new regulations of the United States government. I have a lot of friends who are trying to survive this crisis of having almost no tourism. I believe that if people outside Cuba know how good our food is they will decide to come here one day, and that definitely will help the people. As we say, *We are relatives, we are neighbors, and we love each other.*"

Most of Cuba is still a mystery. I didn't meet any revolutionaries while I was there, and although they do use a home-grown aphrodisiac, I didn't figure out whether it really was a paradise. But I did develop a neighborly love for the country, its inhabitants and their cuisine. Cuba is, as Yamil would say, *full of flavor.* Next time I visit it will be with a full heart, an empty stomach—and my own handsome companion.

Eyes, Wings and Tongues

The Third Eye of the Tuatara

An ancient cannibal skitters toward extinction

On a small island in the South Pacific dwells the strangest of creatures: a cannibal with a crest of spiky spines down the center of its back and tail, three rows of teeth, and invisible ears. It starts out small, but keeps growing larger and larger for the first thirty-five years of its hundred-year life. Scientists have studied the genome of this beast, which suggests it is a freakish amalgamation of lizard, bird and mammal. Oddest of all, to my mind, is its third eye.

This lizard-like reptile, called the tuatara, survives in the wild only in New Zealand. I was headed there, along with my husband Jim, for a conference, and as soon as I heard about the tuatara I was determined to see one.

"We have to figure out a way to see a tuatura while we're in New Zealand," I announced prior to our trip.

"I've done some research."

"I'm sure you have," he replied, peering at me over the top of his glasses. "Let's start with the scientific name." (He knows me really well.)

"*Sphenodon punctatus*. It's a species like no other. Actually, it's a genus, a family, and an order like no other, because it's the sole survivor of the *Rhychocephalia/Sphenodontia* order."

"Your point, Laurie?"

"It's ancient! The tuatara predates even the earliest dinosaurs. All of its closest relatives are fossils."

"So we won't be meeting the whole family then. Is this another one of your wild goose chases ... like the cassowary?"

Ah yes, the cassowary. At my insistence we'd gone on an Australian cassowary hunt and hadn't seen a single one. I wasn't sure we'd see a tuatara either, since it is so rare and lives only on a few small islands off New Zealand's mainland. But viewing one was worth a try. I'd been obsessing about the creature and my research had turned up all kinds of fascinating facts.

Most sensational of these was the story of Henry, a tuatara that became a surprise father at the age of 111 "after receiving treatment for a cancer that had made him hostile toward prospective mates." The UK-based *MailOnline* went on to say that Henry was "caught canoodling with a female named Mildred" and that the pair had produced eleven offspring. An accompanying photo showed Henry and Mildred *in flagrante*.

A casual observer could be forgiven for thinking a tuatara is a lizard. It *looks* like a lizard. Like true lizards it has scaly skin, lays eggs, and eats insects and other invertebrates. But there are significant, if inconspicuous, differences: that third row of teeth, for example. The tuatara's row of bottom teeth fits neatly in between two parallel rows of top choppers, which the tuatara moves in a slicing motion rather than up and down. This gives young tuatara the ability to rip apart hard-bodied insects. It makes the larger adults fearsome predators that can easily decapitate birds, and sometimes even eat their own offspring.

Also unlike lizards, tuatara are nocturnal. This may be because they function best in cool weather (lizards like it warm). In fact, the tuatara has an extremely low optimal body temperature—the lowest of any reptile—and can remain active in near-freezing temperatures.

And then there's my favorite part, the third eye. Situated on top of the tuatara's head and more primitive than a regular eye, it is barely visible. Still, it has a lens, retina, and nerve endings, and is sensitive to light. It turns out that many species of lizards, frogs, and salamanders also have this "parietal eye"; lampreys actually have two. The eye probably helps animals with navigation, thermoregulation and managing circadian rhythms.

I've long been fascinated with the idea of a third eye—as has much of the rest of humankind. In fact, we've linked this enigmatic aperture with the pineal gland and assigned it special importance since ancient times. In pharaonic Egypt, beginning in the thirty-second century BCE, priests associated the pineal gland with the Eye of Horus, a symbol of power, protection and good health. Hindu yogis connected it with Sahasrara, the chakra of enlightenment. Second-century Greeks believed the pineal gland regulated "psychic pneuma," which was "the first instrument of the soul." Seventeenth-century philosopher René Descartes declared it was the source of all thought, as well as the "principal seat of the soul."

In current times, New Age body-mind practitioners like Dr. Joe Dispenza—a chiropractor with post-graduate training in neuroplasticity, epigenetics, and brain/heart coherence—have written about the pineal. Dispenza pointed out in 2017 that if you apply Fibonacci's constant to a cross-section of the human brain, following the resulting spiral along the circumference of that organ, it will end precisely at the pineal gland—signifying, at least, that the pineal must be something very special. Dr. Dispenza describes a method of coordinated breathing and muscle control that he says induces a wave in the cerebrospinal fluid, activating the pineal in a way that primes the brain for mystical experience.

The tuatara fascinates scientists for other reasons, as well. It is uncommonly resistant to infectious diseases. It has an unusually large number of genes involved in protection against cellular aging, which might eventually provide insights that help humans live longer. And x-ray microtomography scans of particular small tuatara bones and cartilage formations are helping morphologists understand the evolution of kneecaps.

One would expect such a remarkable species to be held in great esteem, and in fact it is, by the Māori people, who view the tuatara as a guardian of knowledge and regard it as a *taonga* or special treasure. But despite that esteem—as well as the efforts of New Zealand's Department of Conservation—habitat loss and predation by rats and other introduced pests have led to the tuatara's declining population. Which is why Jim and I were only able to see the tuatara at a zoological park near Wellington, rather than in the wild. Additionally, the tuatara, being nocturnal and very sensitive to light, is not viewable during daylight hours.

"We're going on a night walk," I announced.

"Not another one.

"They're fun. Remember the kiwi?"

"What kiwi?" Our kiwi night walk had been a bust. It had taken several hours, and although we'd heard the bird calling, we saw only its legs and a flash of its hair-like feathers. This promised to be a similar situation, but the strength of my determination won the debate. We had to hang out at a nearly empty wildlife park for several hours after closing time, waiting for darkness to fall. The night was moonless and cold, Jim's feet were hurting, and boredom had set in. So had irrirability. "This had better be worth it," he warned.

When we finally set out, we had to use red-lensed flashlights so as not to disturb the vision of all the nocturnal creatures we were sure to see. Those creatures turned out to be mostly glow worms, which, although magical in their own right, were not the three-eyed cannibals I longed to encounter.

As we walked along the narrow path, deeper and deeper into the forest, dry leaves crackled beneath our feet. A cool breeze gave me the shivers. Jim was right—this had better be worth the trip. I turned to him. "I just want to point out that the tuatara is an amazing creature. It's one of the world's longest living and slowest growing animals. In fact, it's a national icon of slowness."

"If it's so slow, why did they name a race car after it?"

"I don't remember reading anything about race cars. I don't think that's right."

"Yes it is. I've done my research, too. Shelby makes a car called the Tuatara. It's got a top speed of nearly 300 miles an hour."

"Hmmm. A testosterone lover's dream," I mused, poking the bushes with my walking stick. "Speaking of which, did you know that a recent comparison of tuatara embryos with fossil evidence suggests that external male genitalia originated just once in amniotes?" I wasn't sure where I was going with this information, but it sounded interesting.

"Amniotes? What are those?"

"All mammals, birds, lizards, crocodiles ... and tuatara. But external genitalia have since undergone dramatic modification, disappearing altogether in birds and reptiles. There's more. The gender of tuatara, like that of some tortoises, is determined by the temperature of its nest. When incubation temperatures rise above 72°F, tuatara hatchlings all turn out to be males."

"Good if you're a female tuatara," Jim says, raising his left eyebrow suggestively.

"Not so good for the species, though," I counter. I hate it when he wiggles his eyebrow. It makes me want to argue with whatever he has just said. I get right to it. "Climate change is going to be a disaster for them."

As it turns out, we found little to amaze us on that three-hour exploration under the cloak of darkness. No triple rows of teeth. No mysterious third eyes. No dragon-like creatures devouring their own young. What we *were* able to do is watch as two or three small lizards—ok, tuatara—skittered across the dark path in front of us into the shelter of nearby bushes. All were under a foot long—including the tails—and had miniscule rows of nobby spines decorating their necks, backs and tails. They had big eyes that glowed red in the light we provided, and large, expressive forefeet.

And that was the end of our adventure.

I feel sorry for the tuatara. Once widespread, there are now fewer than 80,000 individuals. The youngsters must be wary of being eaten by their parents. They also have the constant problem of attack by rats, and they don't even have real teeth. Instead, their jaws are like saws, with serrations poking out of the jawbone. If the "teeth" break off or are damaged, there's no way for the tuatara to grow them back. And, with their one-hundred-year life-spans, this sad situation is a long one. So, all in all, not the most promising outcome for the bearer of an impressive and mystically celebrated third eye, the last survivor of a genus, species and order.

On the bright side, though, there's Henry—still canoodling at 111.

My Little Red Coquette

Infatuation hums in the rainforest

A broad, wooden verandah at one end of the rain-forest lodge opens onto a sheltered lawn that's lush with flowering bushes and brightly colored birds. I'm at one of my favorite spots in the world, the Asa Wright Nature Center in Trinidad's forested highlands, where you can easily see twenty different avian species in the space of twenty minutes. An ardent birder, I love them all, but my aspiration is to catch a glimpse of *Lophornis ornatus*, the tufted coquette.

I'm not the only one charmed by this little beauty; it's one of the center's star attractions. *Ornatus* refers to the bird's ornate plumage. Like many other hummingbirds, its head, back, and wings are bright green; its tail and wingtips, darker. A pale buff bar crosses the rump. But its most distinguishing features are the male's brilliant vermillion collar and crest—and the adorable black polka dots on tufts along the sides of his neck. It is an exquisite creature, and to a bird lover, catching a glimpse of one is the equivalent of coming upon a rare treasure.

Trinidad is one of the best places in the world for watching birds. More than 400 species have been identified on the island, which is about the size of the state of Delaware. Although small, it has some 40% as many species as the entire United States. But it isn't just Trinidad's species count that's impressive; it's the island's absolute *spectacle* of birds. The rainforest erupts with colorful honeycreepers, orioles, tanagers, and some of the world's most beautiful hummingbirds, easy to identify because the names are conveniently descriptive. The copper-rumped hummer has an emerald face and throat, a dark tail, white "socks" ... and a copper rump. It's the most common visitor here at the feeders, and its territorial behavior is fun to watch. Equally territorial is the male white-necked jacobin, with its gorgeously iridescent dark blue hood in sharp contrast to a bright white belly. And yes, he has a white collar at the back of his neck. The rufous-breasted hermit has a rufous or reddish-bronze throat and paler belly. Its bright chestnut outer tail feathers are tipped in an inky black, then tipped again with a sliver of stark white. Its long beak turns downward, and the two mandibles are different colors: dark gray on top, yellow for the bottom one. When perched, he wags his tail up and down. One of the most inquisitive birds here, the rufous-breasted hermit comes up to within three feet of my face and hovers, observing me as I observe him.

While I'm watching, a spectacled thrush creeps in, meowing like a cat. Black-and-white bananaquits flit in the trees, showing off their bright yellow bellies. Time stands still, and I realize I've been blissing out with these magical little beings for more than an hour.

The center is in Trinidad's northern mountains. Once you've flown to the capital city, Port of Spain, you need to drive for several hours—much of the way on bumpy, rutted roads. My trips to Asa Wright are always worth the trouble, though; it's a heavenly spot. The canopy, in some places, is 150 feet high.

I had already made a couple of excursions from my Asa Wright basecamp. At Caroni Swamp on the island's northwestern coast I climbed into a canoe and navigated through several miles of swampland—dark, dank, and filled with mosquitoes—to see roseate spoonbills. Two hundred or so of the crimson beauties weighed down the branches of a mangrove like bright red ornaments decorating a magical Christmas tree. This alone is a world-class birding experience, but there was much more to come.

Later, driving along a road called John Boodoo

Trace south of the Arima Forest, I spotted what looked like a mass of brown, hairy tube socks hanging from a tall tree. As much as four feet long and six or seven inches wide at the bulbous base, these baskets are handiwork of the crested oropendola, a colonial breeder that weaves nests by the dozens and suspends them from the very tips of branches. I stared, hypnotized, at the swaying nests and the oropendola themselves—big black birds with a bright yellow tail and beak and striking blue eyes.

Back at Asa Wright, I head out on the promisingly named Bellbird Trail, one of several footpaths leading out from the lodge. An easy hike takes me down into deep forest where torch ginger and lobster-claw heliconia, with their bright red and orange flowers, line the pathway. Nutmeg trees, originally from South America but long ago naturalized here, grow behind them, twenty feet tall with tiny yellow flowers. Strangler figs and monkey-ladder vines twist their way skyward. Less light filters through the treetops as the overstory thickens, and the dimness enhances my other senses.

Already the day is hot and humid; moisture in the air mingles with my perspiration. My feet thud an odd, hollow rhythm on the hard dirt path. Each time a breeze wafts through, long stalks of bamboo sway, complaining with languorous sighs. Buzzing insects and melodic birdsong merge in an auditory vapor; I suspect the musicality of the Trinidadian language was born from these lilting rainforest tones.

Overhead, trees echo with the squawk of channel-billed toucans. Lots of them wing their way through the jungle, but the vegetation is so dense you can't see the toucans—you can only hear their harsh, single-syllable call. My field guide describes it as a "high-pitched *pyok*, repeated at intervals of a few seconds; at a distance [it] resembles the yelping bark of a puppy." I can't help but wonder how magical the jungle must have seemed to the author, filled as it was with the sound of flying puppies.

If you *could* see these birds, you'd recognize the toucan often kept as a pet: about twenty inches long, with a mostly-black body, a way-big beak, and a gorgeous, bright orangey-yellow breast. As if their looks weren't enchanting enough, my guidebook goes on to describe their courtship behavior: "The male feeds the female, handing berries in its ungainly bill with remarkable dexterity." So sweet.

I still use my 1980 edition of ffrench's (sic) *A Guide to the Birds of Trinidad and Tobago*—the only comprehensive volume on local birds when I bought it in 1987. It's a hardback, and nearly two inches thick. Nevertheless, it's been worth lugging around, as it's bursting with all kinds of fascinating information, not to mention the fact that the author's unusual name,

Richard P. ffrench—with its double-f and lack of a capital letter—is so intriguing I often find myself wondering about the man. I don't have a regular birding buddy in Trinidad, so Mr. ffrench has become my companion.

I wander deeper into the forest, hoping to sight the bearded bellbird I've heard from the lodge. It's a light-colored, foot-long bird with a dark brown head and wings, and should be easy to spot. The male has an unusual brown "beard" consisting of dark, string-like wattles that hang down from its bare throat. Suddenly I hear the bellbird's echoing call—which sounds somewhat like a bell, hence the name. It beckons, but confuses me. One minute it seems to be nearly overhead; the next it's far away. Is it one bird, or two? Is the bird here, or there?

Turns out it's both. The male cries out with a metallic *bawk* to defend his calling territory. It has an odd resonance that reverberates through the forest like a hammer hitting an anvil. I consult my ffrench's and learn that the male regularly turns "to face a new direction, and he tends to call when a neighbor is nearby." No wonder I'm baffled. I'm apparently in the midst of dueling male ventriloquists, each turning to project his voice in a circle around his territory. The loudest caller gets the female, assuming he already has his beard. No beard, no chance. I finally find the male, perched on a branch perhaps thirty-five feet above the trail, and am surprised that he lets me get close enough to clearly see his magnificent wattles. I'm disappointed not to witness the bellbird's display preening, in which he "shows off ... a patch of bare skin on the thigh." Or so Mr. ffrench says.

A branching trail leads to the reserve's famous oilbirds, which I hear long before I see them. Screams and squawks fill the air, along with the distinct sound of vomiting. It's an awful racket, accompanied by a nasty odor. I scramble over rocks and stop at the entrance to the dim cave.

Up at the lodge, someone said these creatures are called oilbirds because so much of their body is fat, and that they were once commonly speared on the end of a sturdy stick by indigenous people and lighted on fire to form a torch. Consequently, there aren't many left—but the colony here is flourishing. In fact, one of the original reasons the Asa Wright Nature Center was founded was to help protect these rare birds.

I consult Mr. ffrench for an explanation. The oilbirds, he says, were used by locals as a source of fuel for cooking and light. No specific mention of the torches. He also says they are nocturnal, eating fruit they pluck from trees in flight, at night, which they're able to do because they navigate like bats using echolocation. They later disgorge the seeds and use the resulting vomit to make their nests, which are "constructed mainly of regurgitated fruit forming a paste." Ah—that explains the noise, and the smell.

The cave is not a pleasant place to visit. In addition to the incessant retching and the odor that accompanies it, there's the matter of my having disturbed the birds, even though I'm keeping my distance. They're huge—with three-and-a-half-foot wingspans—which is particularly distressing when they are flapping restlessly in the confines of their narrow, cramped cave. I decide to spare the birds and myself any further torment, and head back for the trail.

I'm hoping for an antidote to the chaotic oilbird experience, and find it in the golden-headed manakin lek that's right along the path. A lek is an area where male birds gather to compete with one another in their mating rituals. These dancing birds are only about three-and-a-half inches long, with tails so short they're barely noticeable. They sport jet-black bodies, bright yellow heads, a short pink beak, and pink legs. A white ring circles each eye, giving the impression of bespectacled intelligence—until you see the males' strange, Michael Jackson-moonwalk-like mating dance. It's such a silly show that it gives me the giggles, and I need to move along so I don't scare the birds away.

But the afternoon is sweltering, so I'm happy to head back to the lodge where I can relax with a rum punch and watch the hummingbirds buzz around the feeders. I've been here for two days, but still haven't seen my little red coquette. After searching for so long, I think of the bird as "mine," in the same way my mother-in-law, who had a crush on the actor James Garner, always refered to him as "my" James Garner. Unilateral infatuation has made the little red coquette *mine*.

Out on the verandah, the air is filled with sweet, high-pitched tweets, and the feathery flashes of sapphire and green, red, topaz and purple zip by. They call to mind Einstein's Special Theory of Relativity, which suggests that time slows down as speed increases. What does that mean for these tiny birds, whose hearts beat some 1,200 times each minute? Even their wings vibrate faster than the human eye can see—up to eighty times a second. I try to imagine what I must look like to the rufous-breasted hermit as it hovers so close I feel the rush of air from its wings. Does time bend when it flies? Do I appear to move slowly when the bird is whizzing through the air, but more quickly when it's hovering? Do I seem barely animate, like trees look to humans?

The sun begins to sink, and the hummers are off to bed. I'm up early the next morning, sitting at the far end of the porch, just across from a big bush full of red flowers. I've heard it's the tufted coquette's favorite spot. Rather than venturing into the bushes, I sit as quietly as possible; this is the best way to sight a shy hummer.

The other birds fly in and out: yellow-and-black orioles; purple and green honeycreepers; cocoa woodcreepers; gray-fronted doves; an assortment of blue-gray, bay-headed, white-shouldered, and silver-beaked tanagers; the purple-backed and famously musical violaceous euphonia with its sunny yellow chest and forehead. Hummingbirds are also out in full force: white-chested emeralds, black-throated mangoes, blue-chinned sapphires, long-billed starthroats.

Finally, around 9:30 in the morning, the female tufted coquette appears. She's so tiny and quick that at first I mistake her for a giant bumblebee. At just over two-and-a-half inches—including her tail—she's one of the world's smallest birds. She's paler than a male and lacks some of his distinctive field marks, but her tiny size and a prominent white band across her rump make identification easy. She buzzes from flower to flower, never staying long in one place, and spends altogether too much time hidden on the far side of the bush—a true coquette.

Then the male appears and honest-to-gosh, my heart catches. He is spectacular: iridescent green, with a magnificent vermillion crest that pokes up nearly an inch from his forehead like a bright crown. Long, pale scarlet plumes stretch backwards from his cheeks and over his shoulders. The feathers are of varying lengths and each is tipped with a dark green-black splotch, giving the tufts their polka-dotted look. He can flatten the tufts in against his body or project them out from the sides of his neck in an exquisite display—which he does several times, hovering just a few feet away. For several seconds I am overwhelmed by his beauty.

Finally, I relax. I have hunted down the roseate spoonbill colony and the elusive bellbird. I watched the golden-headed manakins dance and heard the rare oilbirds retch. I enjoyed the magic of sitting still as sparkling hummingbirds hovered silently, or whizzed by, or chased competitors away from the feeder. And I learned an exhilarating lesson about birdwatching and life: Sometimes, if you put yourself in the right place at the right time, and have a bit of patience, you don't have to search for treasure—it will fly right up to you and say hello.

The Great Bald Eagle Fly-In at Klamath Basin

Snow, scavengers, and sex in the sky

Each winter, just as surely as frost laces the trees and ice begins to silence the wetlands, hundreds of bald eagles congregate in a "fly-in" at northern California's Klamath Basin. The best time to see them is during the mid-February peak, when as many as five hundred of the raptors gather there. The weather is numbing.

The fly-in is supposed to be one of the most spectacular events a wildlife enthusiast will ever witness. An enthusiast, that is, who doesn't mind driving hundreds of miles from her cozy home in San Francisco into the boondocks at the northern California border, or staying overnight in an unpainted cinderblock duck-hunting lodge with teeny, tiny, mostly ineffectual heaters and no ensuite bathrooms. One who is willing to rise before dawn and brave subfreezing temperatures.

That wildlife enthusiast would be me.

Bald eagles are awe-inspiring creatures. Their eyesight is said to be so sharp they can see a fish from a mile away, or a rabbit from two miles. They easily climb to 10,000 feet in the air, and reach speeds of one hundred miles an hour in a dive. They can carry the heaviest load of any bird.

We haven't always treated the bald eagles well, despite their raw power and fierce behavior—and not to mention that they're our national emblem. In the early eighteenth century they were a common sight on much of the continent, where as many as half a million lived. But Americans hunted the magnificent birds. We shot them and trapped them and poisoned them. We disrupted their habitat and food supplies. We polluted the environment with DDT, severely impairing the eagles' ability to reproduce. By the 1950s, barely four hundred nesting pairs remained in the lower forty-eight states.

The Bald Eagle Protection Act of 1940 and the Endangered Species Preservation Act of 1966 helped turn the tide, and banning the use of DDT in the United States in 1972 saved our national bird from extirpation. Today there are as many as 10,000 nesting pairs in the lower forty-eight states—and northern California's Klamath Basin is one of the best places to see them.

How could anyone resist the opportunity to see hundreds of these magnificent raptors up close?

So, one icy day in early February I drove north to the Lower Klamath National Wildlife Refuge near the California-Oregon border. The reserve, established by President Theodore Roosevelt in 1908 as the nation's first waterfowl refuge, is now a National Historic Landmark. More than three hundred avian species—ducks, geese, swans, cranes, other waterfowl and shorebirds—wing their way through, part of the fall migration of one million birds. As I drove, the sky occasionally darkened with flocks of honking geese.

The Klamath Basin, an immense expanse of wetlands, meadows, shallow lakes and craggy cliffs, seems breathtakingly vast and fantastically ferocious at this time of year. Remains of carcasses—it's rarely clear what animal they once were—litter the snow-covered grassland. Eagles huddle in the snowy fields, others soar skyward, still others dive from the heavens. The birds are enthralling. Often immature eagles, less able hunters, try to steal scraps from older, more experienced birds. It's easy to ID the immature birds by plumage as well as behavior; bald eagles don't develop their distinctive white head and tail feathers until they are four or five years old. Eventually these young birds will need to learn to catch their own food if they're going to make it through the year.

I was eager to witness the eagles' unforgettable courtship ritual. A pair will climb so high they are nearly invisible, circling one another with elaborate swoops and chases. Then the two birds lock talons and cartwheel head-over-tail, plummeting in a death-defying freefall. At the very last moment before crashing to earth they separate and glide off in apparent nonchalance. When an observer is able to breathe again, it's generally with an awestruck gasp. Eagle sex must be amazing.

In fact everything about eagles is amazing. I'm not the only person to think so—the fierce raptor was emblematic for the Babylonian, Egyptian, and Roman empires. Christian, Aztec, and Muslim texts include it as a spiritual symbol. Eagles represent courage, strength and vision for many Native Americans. And the bald eagle has been the national emblem of the United States since 1782.

Eagles still fascinate people all around the world. A dozen raptor fanatics stayed in the spartan duck-hunting lodge that night. Unlike me, the others were not first-timers. Most had driven up from the San Francisco Bay Area, but one couple was from Europe. There's something irresistible about eagles' power and grace that attracts birdwatchers year after year.

The next morning we gulped hot coffee together in the parking lot before heading out. Tufts of dead grass crunched beneath our feet, ice coated the pavement, and snow blanketed the hillsides. Our breath turned to clouds in the frigid air. It was a daunting start, but

I was game. Locals say the colder the weather, the more eagles there are.

Up well before sunrise, we drove miles of backroads through early-morning darkness to reach a particular spot we had been told was the eagles' night roost, a deciduous forest on a sheltered slope. The bare-branched trees provide easy perching, roosting, takeoffs, and landings for eagles that cluster here at night.

Our source had been a good one. Stark black skeleton-like trees stood outlined against a pale hillside. And on their branches, shadows—the promise of what we had come to see. We didn't need daylight to ID them. The dark brown bodies and snow-white head-and-tail feathers of adults, along with their impressive size—average wingspans approach seven feet—made the raptors unmistakable.

Slowly, the dim light brightened. One bird rose, then another. Soon hundreds of majestic eagles ascended in the thin post-dawn air. I watched in awe as they labored silently upward one by one, then wheeled together in a "kettle" of more than fifty individuals, spiraling in a lazy vortex on a rising thermal. They were surveying the land below, looking for food.

Dozens more loitered in treetops and on the ground less than one hundred yards from the road, occasionally scrapping with each other for morsels of

scavenged food. Eating will be their main job for the coming weeks. Flying in from as far away as Alaska and the Yukon—some have traveled well over a thousand miles—requires a lot of energy. But the rewards of wintering in Klamath's extensive shallow marshes and grassy uplands, where nearly two million waterfowl find food and shelter, are great: fish and ducks are easy prey.

There's also the matter of the calves. Bald eagles are predators, but we've heard the raptors also work as a clean-up crew here in cattle country, feasting on nutritious afterbirth when they come across it during the bitter cold of calving season.

My hands and feet grew numb as we watched for hours. There was plenty of time to talk with other eagle-watchers, many of whom had brought along giant spotting scopes—telescope-like lenses mounted on tripods—perfect for training on one position so we could view the relatively stationary birds. I connected with one guy, Walt, with a particularly big scope and no apparent friends. Lots of birders are loners.

"That's quite a scope you've got there."

"Sure, take a look!" Walt knew what I was after.

"Thanks." I peered through the eyepiece. Walt had the scope trained on a beautiful adult with a bright white head. The eagle was ripping at what looked like the remains of a rabbit; there was surprisingly little blood. "Whoa! We're watching the circle of life here."

"Yep." Walt pulled a wad of waxed paper from the pocket of his parka, unwrapped a sandwich, and took a bite.

A man of few words, I thought, turning back to the scope. "How did you get into birding, Walt?"

"You don't want to know."

"Sure I do. Tell me the story."

What I expected was a story like my own. I've loved birds as long as I can remember; my theory is that it's because my mother hung a mobile with birds on it over my crib, and somehow imprinted me with that connection. I read that Frank Lloyd Wright's mother decorated his nursery with pictures of cathedrals, and that's why he became an architect. But Walt's story was nothing like that.

"I shot a bird once," he said.

I didn't look up from the scope. This seemed like a conversation best had at a distance, an emotional distance anyway, not eye-to-eye. But Walt did not continue.

"And?" I kept my head down. The eagle continued ripping at the carcass, using both feet to hold it down. He ripped off fur, muscle, stringy entrails, and ate it all. He was fast.

"My next-door neighbor, Dennis, we called him Denny, had a BB gun, and we were out playing with it one day. He gave me the gun and told me to shoot a pigeon. I had never even held a gun before, and I didn't want to shoot it, but Denny said I was a sissy—no offense—if I couldn't shoot a pigeon."

"No offense taken. So you shot it?" I glanced at Walt. Suddenly, *not* looking at him seemed too intimate—as though I was making too big a deal of his story. Plenty of kids shot birds with BB guns.

"I didn't kill it, but I shot it down off the telephone wire. We ran over and looked at it, and it was lying on its side, staring up at us with one eye." Walt's voice wavered a little, and I wondered whether he had ever told this story before. I wanted to check for a wedding ring—surely he would have told his wife—but his hands were jammed into his pockets. "Denny grabbed the gun from me and shot it in the head."

"Was that traumatic?" It seemed like an obvious question, and I didn't want to avoid it.

"I never touched a gun again."

"And now you're watching eagles."

"A pigeon is a dove," Walt said, unwilling to move on. "The bird of peace." He lapsed into a world deep with memories.

After that we communed with the eagles in snowy silence: the graceful show as they rose effortlessly into the sky; the slow, dizzying spiral of their kettles; the heart-stopping eagle sex. Walt's spotting scope remained trained on the field in front of us, magnifying the astonishing power of huge, bloody beaks and strong talons as these carnivores ripped at the frozen remains of lesser creatures. I was fascinated, in a secret place in my heart, with such majestic carnage. I could only wonder what Walt was feeling.

Domesticating Janet

On the ethics of riding a two-ton orphan

"Put your hand in the elephant's mouth," Daniel suggests. Although he only comes up to my waist, Rastus, the baby elephant, weighs 340 pounds. He's big enough to knock me over. Big enough to crush me, actually.

I'm visiting a small compound in Zimbabwe where orphaned elephants are fed, sheltered, bathed, and given a home. Five-month-old Rastus is one of them. So is six-year-old Janet, whom I'm about to meet. Daniel is one of the *mahouts*, or elephant handlers, who work at the compound. He's in his twenties and wears park-service-green shorts and a khaki short-sleeved shirt. A green baseball cap protects his eyes from the African sun.

I'm afraid to put my hand in Rastus' mouth, so I stall for time.

"His ears are amazing!" I pet one gently. It's huge, much bigger than the elephant's head. The back side is like a cabbage leaf—smooth and veined. Elegantly curved, it's warm and velvety. Everywhere else, Rastus feels soft and a little hairy.

"Elephants use their ears to regulate temperature. That's why they're so large—to provide surface area."

"Um, does Rastus have teeth?" I peer at his mouth, but it's closed.

"Not yet. He's still teething; his first set of molars will break through in the next month or so."

I remember when my son was a teething baby—the sharp ridges on his front teeth pushing through tender gums, his incessant drooling and relentless need to gnaw, the surprising strength of his bite and hardness of his gums. I won't go as far as saying it hurt me more than it hurt him, but teething is not something I want to experience on an elephantine scale.

"We found Rastus abandoned in the jungle," Daniel says, looking down at his charge. "His mother must have been dead. If we hadn't brought him here, Rastus would've been eaten by a lion or a hyena, or he'd have starved to death. All the elephants here would be dead if they hadn't been rescued."

"He's way too young to find his own food, right?"

"Yeah, these little babies depend on their mothers' milk until they're two years old." Daniel pats Rastus' head.

Rastus lies down on the sparse crabgrass lawn, and Daniel sits next to him. The elephant rolls onto his side and puts his head in Daniel's lap. Then he reaches up and wraps his trunk around Daniel's neck, as though he's throwing an arm around his best friend's shoulder. Which, in a way, he is.

I sit down next to the two pals. "Rastus seems very attached to you."

"Yes, elephants are social animals. A baby growing up in the wild would be within touching distance of his mother all the time."

"How do they interact in captivity?"

"The adult females here love Rastus, especially the young ones. They fawn over him like teenaged girls playing with a cute little baby. But he's bonded to humans because we feed him. He needs to be with someone 24/7."

"Really? What about at night?"

"Rastus is a typical baby; he won't sleep alone."

"How long do they sleep at night?"

"They lie down for about two hours, and you won't believe how loud they are."

I try to imagine the elephants' sleeping sounds—maybe an occasional grunt or sigh, their bodies heaving as they roll over or rearrange a leg, the hay beneath them scratching and rustling. But that's not the kind of noise Daniel is referring to.

"Elephants snore very loudly!" he explains, laughing. "The adults sleep over there in the stable, where they can touch and talk to each other through bars. But they can't get to each others' food—we don't want fights. During the day they might doze resting against a tree, to relieve some of the weight of their tusks."

"How big do their tusks get?" I glance around the compound. A dozen or so elephants mill about in a small stable. An equal number of mahouts, all dressed like Daniel, watch the elephants closely.

"Years ago, an average elephant tusk weighed about a hundred pounds—per side!

"That's a lot of weight to carry around. But these don't look all that big."

"Well, the tusk extends up into the head, so only half of it shows. Also, hunters have killed the animals with the largest tusks, eliminating them from the gene pool. Now the average tusk weighs only about forty pounds. The elephants are losing the tools they need to eat bark."

I'm alarmed to realize we humans have not only encroached on elephants' habitat, not only killed individuals for their ivory tusks, but have also actually influenced their evolutionary path, effectively selecting the smaller-tusked animals for reproduction. I have lots more questions, but Rastus snuggles up next to me and nuzzles me with his trunk. Like a human baby, he needs attention—and demands it.

Caring for these orphans is clearly a big job. "Just feeding him must take a long time," I observe. Rastus drinks milk every few minutes from the liter bottle Daniel offers him. It's topped with a thumb-sized nipple, and Rastus is a good sucker. "How much does he drink?"

"Forty to fifty liters of milk—every day."

"Elephant milk?"

"No; we don't have access to that. We feed Rastus a mixture of nonfat cows' milk and dessicated coconut, with added calcium and multi-vitamins. It's easy to digest and provides plenty of calories. We had to do a lot of experimentation to get the formula right."

"Couldn't you get the recipe from a zoo somewhere?"

"Not really. The success rate—all around the world—for raising baby elephants without their mothers is very low. We're doing surprisingly well here."

I'm trying to take notes, but Rastus will have none of it. He reaches over and fondles my arm with his trunk—snuggling and nuzzling, rubbing and bumping his head against me. I'm smitten.

Daniel can see that the elephant is comfortable with me. "Go ahead; put your hand in his mouth."

I screw up my courage and slide my right hand, palm down, into Rastus' open mouth. That's easier than it sounds, because even a baby elephant's mouth is quite large. It's warm and soft and almost dry inside, not wet and slobbery like I'd expected. Rastus chomps down and gums my hand—just like a human baby that's teething, only not as rough. It's as though the elephant knows he has to be gentle with a human being.

Rastus continues gumming my hand, obviously enjoying himself.

"It's almost time for the elephants to go for their walk," Daniel says, standing abruptly. "Do you want to ride one?"

I'm not sure about this for a number of reasons. "Is it hard?" I ask.

"No, it's easy. And the elephants don't mind. Robert is a mahout; he will take you; I'll stay with Rastus." I wonder how Daniel knows whether or not the elephants mind. He probably sees the question in my expression. "Don't worry. We train them very gently—not like Indian elephants."

I hadn't realized Asian and African elephants were trained differently, and consider whether it might have to do with the elephants' temperaments or with differing traditions of training—or with the trainers themselves. I don't worry much about it at this point however, because something else is on my mind. I don't want to leave Rastus. *He's my baby!* I think, as he snuggles up against my leg. *I can't leave my baby.*

But Rastus is back to gumming Daniel's hand. He's Daniel's baby, not mine. My heart drops as I turn toward Robert, and we walk over to the elephant I will ride.

"This is Janet," Robert says, introducing us.

Janet has gigantic ears—one of them would easily wrap around my body like a blanket. My head comes up to her yellowing tusks, which are brighter at their points than at the base where they intersect with her thick skin. The left tusk is half a yard long; the right one is shorter—closer to a foot. Their ends taper to blunt points just inches from my face. Janet's own face is criss-crossed with a vaguely geometric pattern of wrinkles. A dark smear of dampness escapes from the inner corners of her tiny eyes. Her expression is impenetrable.

"She's kind of small ..."

"Janet's six years old," Robert says. "Get on. It's easy."

I step over grassy clods of elephant dung, climb a tall, sturdy mounting platform and finally swing my leg over Janet's back. She wears a leather saddle, like a horse's, only elephant-sized. Robert scrambles up after me but sits in front of the saddle, just behind Janet's ears.

We sway along in a slow caravan with a dozen other elephants, all about the same size, each with a passenger and a mahout. A half-mile loop leads us through the veld to a small lake and then back again. Janet and the other elephants stop frequently to browse on clumps of grass or leafy branches. At the lake they mill around the muddy bank, slurping drinks among the reeds and lilypads. The mahouts don't pressure or hurry them, and the elephants seem comfortable. Actually, they seem much more amenable to carrying passengers than many horses I've known.

"Why is Janet's left tusk longer than her right one?"

"Are you right handed, or left-handed?"

"What?"

"Elephants are like humans; they are either right-tusked or left-tusked. The tusks get a lot of use—digging up trees and stripping branches—and the one that's used most gets worn down. Fortunately, they keep growing until the elephant is about thirty-five years old."

"What's an elephant's life span, anyway?"

"It depends on their teeth."

"Did you say their *teeth*?" I wasn't sure I'd heard him right.

"Like us, elephants have more than one set of teeth. Actually, they get six sets. Their final molars will come in before they're fifty. When those wear down, maybe in ten years, the elephants starve to death."

I'd never thought about the end of life for an elephant. I look down at Janet, wondering about the quality of her life so far. Some people say it's cruel for humans to ride elephants, and I hope I'm not rationalizing in thinking it's similar to riding a horse. That doesn't seem cruel. Is the difference that horses are domesticated, but elephants are not? In the long run, that doesn't seem like much of an issue; the process takes generations. And after all, horses were wild once, too.

"Do they mind giving us rides?" I ask Robert.

"They give visitors a ride, and visitors pay for their upkeep. The elephants work for a living, just like we do."

These elephants are tame; they've been trained to accept the presence of humans, and even to let us ride them. But they haven't been *domesticated*—that would mean yet another a genetic modification, like the length of their tusks, one that led to an inherited predisposition toward humans.

The process of domestication may seem unnatural, but what if the animal *itself* initiates domestication—does that change anything? Evolutionary biologists believe that when dogs began to diverge from wolves, some 15,000 years ago, it was a process initiated by the wolves, not by humans. Wolves that came closest to human encampments got more food, which encouraged them to spend even more time near humans, which got them more food, which meant stronger wolves that became better breeders—and so it went. Cats were the same, except that they domesticated themselves much later, after we had developed agriculture and graneries. For cats, rats were the gateway to domestication.

My father believed one of a parent's primary responsibilities is to "break" a child of its wildness, like trainers break horses to the saddle. In both cases, it's in the service of helping the child/horse develop the correct behaviors to allow it to function effectively in its environment. I didn't think that way when I raised my son, but what about the way I'm treating Janet? Have I participated in domesticating her, or her lineage? If so, is that wrong? Does the fact that she was a rescue animal make any difference? I don't know.

What I do know is that my association with the elephants here in Zimbabwe—Rastus, Janet and the others—has increased my appreciation for this magnificent species. Elephants play, cooperate, teach each other, and learn. They appear to experience joy, grief, jealousy, empathy, and compassion; to have a conception of death; and even to die—from what's been described as "broken heart syndrome"—when separated from their social group.

We humans have interacted with elephants for

millennia—or should I say we have *used* them? We have turned them into war machines and beasts of burden. We have saddled them, taught them circus tricks, hunted them for ivory, shot at them for sport and taxidermied them as marksmen's trophies. We have encroached on their homeland and destroyed their habitat—and we're in the process of decimating the very planet they live on.

Even now, back at home and halfway around the globe, I often think of Janet and Rastus. What will their world be like in fifty years? What do elephants gain in this process of domestication? What do they give up? What do we all gain and lose when we sublimate our wildness in order to live closer together in a shrinking world?

Body Works

The Fat Ladies of Malta

A goddess, a couch, and a sacred nap

A mere speck in the Mediterranean Sea, the island of Malta is home to a host of hefty women, often referred to as the Fat Ladies of Malta. Let me hasten to explain that these are not real, living ladies, but rather a collection of female figures, molded from clay or carved from stone and ranging from pocket-sized amulets to mammoth effigies nearly ten feet tall. These ladies are ancient. The temple sites where they were found are older than the Greek Parthenon or the Palace at Knossos, older than the Great Pyramids at Giza ... older, even, than Stonehenge—they are the oldest known freestanding stone monuments in the entire world. The Fat Ladies are found all over the island, and archaeologists have long pondered their meaning.

I was in Malta on a layover and decided I had to see

some of these figures for myself. My destination? A 6,000-year-old catacomb called the Hal Saflieni Hypogeum. The word *hypogeum*—for those of us with a tenuous grasp of Greek—simply means *underground*. This particular hypogeum is a vast, multi-level maze of subterranean chambers, many of which were used for burials; as many as 7,000 people were once interred in its labyrinthine depths. The underground complex is now a UNESCO World Heritage site, and sitting directly over it is a museum that's home to one of the world's masterpieces of prehistoric sculpture: a ceramic Fat Lady called the Sleeping Lady of Hal Saflieni.

A little pre-trip research revealed that the Sleeping Lady is an iconic representation of either death or the afterlife. Or she may be a fertility goddess. Or, most likely, she is demonstrating the spiritual practice of incubation. At any rate, she is a seriously significant piece of Neolithic art, and I was dying to have a look.

But first I had to find her. When I asked about the Hypogeum's location I was invariably directed to the nearby Tarxien Temple complex—not the place I'd asked about. A shopkeeper said, "You turn left at the corner. Then you turn left again..." But she pointed to the right. I asked a woman on the street for directions, but she discouraged me, saying, "You don't want to go to the museum; it's a long walk. Ten or fifteen minutes." She, too, directed me to the Tarxien Temples —so that was my first stop.

It was immediately clear why they'd sent me: The largest of Malta's stone deities dominates the outside court of Tarxien's South Temple.* Unfortunately, only her lower half survives, but from the waist down this goddess is magnificent. Her buttocks are supernaturally proportioned, her pleated skirt playful, her bloomers delightfully voluminous, and her tiny feet, although severely overburdened, are elegant. The oldest known anthropomorphic statue from Mediterranean prehistory, this goddess stands among sturdy stone walls, carefully partitioned temple apses, fallen lintels carved with rhythmic leaves and vines, right-angled cubbyholes, decorated stone screens, a hearth, a huge bowl hewn from a single boulder, and friezes depicting goats, pigs, a bull, and Malta's distinctive version of a divine spiral. There was so much fascinating rubble in this open-air museum that I wandered for hours, happy to be alone and lost in fantasies of the Neolithic world and all the promise it brought: the agricultural revolution, permanent dwellings, domesticated animals...

It was extremely hot that October in Malta, and the sunburn on the back of my neck reminded me it was time to head over to the Hypogeum. Entrance to the catacombs is strictly limited. Only ten people per hour are allowed inside. I secured a ticket and climbed down a winding staircase with my group, descending into beautifully carved rooms that had been there for nearly six millennia. A guide told us about the considerable technical skill required to carve this underground masterpiece, especially since the people had no metal tools, but I was unable to absorb the details. The rock was strong, yet its edges were soft. The light was dim but strategically directed. The rhythmic repetition of posts and lintels drew me deeper and deeper into the chambers until I was surrounded by smooth, cool walls I sensed more than saw, and overwhelmed with that particular kind of awe ancient history inspires. I was reluctant to leave such an intensely magical place, but soon our underground hour was over; it was time to explore the museum above the catacombs.

When I found the Sleeping Lady I was sorely disappointed. She may have been one of Malta's Fat Ladies, but she was small—less than five inches long. I had been looking for another giant statue, and almost missed her! It wasn't crowded so I put my nose against the glass case for a closer look. And that's when my admiration began to blossom. Unashamedly corpulent in proportion, she is a voluptuous masterpiece modeled from clay, colored with Italian ochre and baked to a rosy ceramic. The 5,000-year-old goddess lies on her right side, right leg bent slightly at the knee, arm raised at the shoulder and crooked at the elbow to cradle her head. She relaxes on an elegant piece of furniture resembling a fainting couch, with a low back and a slim mattress. The couch is slightly curved, like the clamshell in Botticelli's *Birth of Venus*, and is supported by four knobby legs.

The Sleeping Lady's own legs, by comparison, are huge. They are hidden by a long skirt, form-fitting from the waist to her knees where it bursts into rhythmic pleats that end just above her delicate ankles. She wears an apron, tied around her waist and falling to just above the pleats. It looks the like the aprons my grandmothers wore in their kitchens.

Lovely as the Sleeping Lady's lower half is, it's her upper body that is spellbinding. She is unclothed on top and her full breasts—each larger than her head—are mostly hidden by her left arm, which rests languorously across them. *That arm is what undoes me.* Bearing no trace of musculature, it is exuberantly obese—and undeniably beautiful. The upper arm is spherical—like a big, summer-ripe casaba, echoed by the smaller sphere that is the figure's head and the larger one that is her hip. Her forearm resembles a plump turkey leg.

The artful rhythm and proportion of the Sleeping Lady's form leave no doubt of the sculptor's talent—even though she's under five inches long, this lady was *meant* to be big. What is in doubt, however, is the figure's meaning. Scholars have suggested that the position of the Sleeping Lady and the fact that she is reclining on a couch, rather than in a bed, suggest that she depicts the rite of incubation, in which a person makes an offering to a god or goddess, sleeps in a sacred place, and prays for a divinely inspired dream or cure. The result was often alleviation of suffering and a heightened sense of intimacy, and even unity, with the deity.

Although incubation was widely practiced throughout the Mediterranean in ancient times (especially by the cult of Asclepius), we'll never really know what the sculptor intended. It's intriguing—the idea of incubation as an affirmation of the feminine yin, of patience and receptivity as avenues for connecting with the divine. And because the Sleeping Lady was found in the most sacred part of the temple complex—an inner chamber called the *Holy of Holies*—it's likely that incubation was an important religious ritual.

I'd heard there was another woman. This time I had a map, and trudged through the heat to the National Museum of Archaeology in search of a sculpture called the Venus of Malta. Even older than the Sleeping Lady, she is a big-breasted figure reminiscent of the famous Venus of Willendorf, but more realistic looking. This Fat Lady, too, is a skillfully sculpted beauty, with special attention to prominent shoulder blades and voluptuous buttocks. And like the Sleeping Lady, she's a miniature. A whole cache of miniature Fat Lady figurines was found near the Venus; they're believed to have been used in temple rituals.

What is remarkable to me about these pieces is that many are definitively squashed. It's as though the figures were modeled in three dimensions then laid on their backs and carefully compressed with a heavy object and even pressure, so that they are still 3D, but flattened. They look quite a bit like a breast undergoing a mammogram. They also remind me of the present-day work of painter Jenny Saville, whose astonishing *Closed Contact* series shows her own zaftig body naked and flattened as though it's been squashed against the glass of a giant copy machine.

All these figures are a revelation for me. They are beautiful in the way a Flemish Rubens or a Colombian Botero is beautiful, without regard for the scrawny stylishness that's popular today. I wish I had seen the Fat Ladies of Malta when I was a girl, when I was finding my way in the world of fashion magazines and gym classes, when my young and impressionable psyche was steeped in the toxic beauty standards and body shaming that are so prevalent in our culture.

Those Fat Ladies of Malta would have inspired me to value the strength and solidity, the languor and fluidity, the shapely and generous beauty of an ample figure. The Sleeping Lady would have been proof positive that my natural inclination toward contemplation—and naps—was perfectly acceptable. Finally, many years later, these ladies have given me permission to fully accept both my shape and my disposition. What a relief! Pass the pasta; I'm headed for the couch.

* Many of the sculptures I thought I was seeing "*in situ*" were actually very good copies of the originals, which are ensconced in pristine, temperature- and humidity-controlled glass cases at Malta's National Museum of Archaeology in Valetta.

said to contain a witch
an old lady living in a
village near Hove, Sussex
Pres. by Miss M.A. Murray, 1926

The Curious Case of the Witch in a Bottle and Other Illuminating Oddities

Should I pop the cork?

The Pitt Rivers Museum in Oxford houses an extensive collection of ethnographic articles from around the world, and has lured me in for a visit. I have come especially to see one particular item, the "Witch in a Bottle." How could I not? I read about it in a guidebook, and once you hear about a thing like that your curiosity builds up and builds up—at least mine does—until you have so many questions you can't stand it: *What kind of bottle? What kind of witch? Has anyone ever opened the bottle? Is the witch's black cat in there with her? And what about the pointy hat—how did they get* that *to fit in?*

The museum is easy to locate, but the witch is not; after wandering for fifteen minutes in the cavernous-but-gloomy main hall I cannot find any sign of the remarkable artifact. Truth be told, I was lost as soon as I entered the room, which is said to be the actual chamber that served as inspiration for the magic shop where Harry Potter bought his sorcery supplies—including magic wands.

The antique wood-and-glass cases are packed with every imaginable kind of exotica, from bright green parrot-feather aprons to ancient bagpipes made from a sheepskin, with the natural leg openings leading to the pipes. Items addressing the most basic challenges of civilization—methods of making fire, tools for tallies and counting, headrests and pillows—crowd together in the murky shadows. Next-level coping mechanisms like snuff-taking equipment languish next to voice disguisers and gambling accoutrements. Even without the witch in a bottle the room would be, well, spellbinding. Expecting dark dementors to descend from the second-story gallery at any minute, I silently prepare to call up my Patronus Charm.

Wandering to the far side of the room, I come upon an entire wall devoted to primping—not crucial for the advancement of civilization, perhaps, but definitely useful in certain social situations. The cases overflow with ancient Roman sweat scrapers, Malaysian head-flattening boards, and ear-cleaning implements from several cultures. Buttocks ornaments, ingenious devices for hair removal, and various tools for tattooing and scarification flank British breast implants from the

1960s and other inventive methods for reshaping, revamping and redesigning the human body for maximum impact. It's a collection of precursors to the tools of modern beauty.

All these items fascinate, but what I am particularly drawn to is the display of flamboyant masks from southeast Nigeria, which also includes a complete costume "used to detect witches." Its crocodile-like mask sports two heads, four-foot-long hair made of a raffia-like material, and several dozen huge feathers jutting out dramatically from the top scalp. The feathers, which were plucked from a nocturnal bird called the great plantain eater, "enable the pursuit of witches in flight at night … especially [important] in maintaining men's control over the affairs of women." Yes, that certainly sounds like a witch hunt. The witch in a bottle must be nearby …

But I still haven't found it, so I approach the only other person in the room: a docent. This man is just over six feet tall, hunches a bit, and stands so still I'm not entirely certain he isn't an exhibit, himself. His nametag says *William*, and, as I approach, I notice that William smells strongly of stale cigarette smoke. He is dressed completely in shades of gray that compliment his aroma.

"Hello. Can you tell me where to find the witch in a bottle?"

Clearly happy to have an audience—even an

audience of one—William pulls a dishwater-colored hankie out of his pants pocket, pats his lips, and begins, "That's been our most popular exhibit; it's really what the Pitt Rivers Museum is all about."

I may have just uncovered a crown jewel, but I'm surprised at William's characterization. "The museum is all about witches?"

"It's about the fact that people have the same problems everywhere," William explains. "They solve them in different ways. Maybe they have metal; maybe they don't. By the way, don't miss the recycling exhibit on the second floor."

Maybe they have metal? This statement is a total mystery. William has apparently been standing alone for a very long time, speaking to no one. I would expect at least a paragraph about the merits of metal, but William leaves it at one sentence. And since he has moved on to recycling so quickly, I follow suit.

"What kind of recycling?"

"It's examples of practical repurposing, using materials at hand." He waves his own hand toward the stairway. "You'll see an oil lamp made from a talcum powder can and a rat trap made from Fujicolor film canisters. My favorites are the blue glass arrowheads made by Australian Aboriginals from discarded cold-cream jars." William nods toward another exhibit. "Over there you'll find a chimpanzee necklace made of hair and vegetable matter."

Vegetable matter? William is proving to be as inscrutable as the exhibits. I picture a length of plump green peas, strung together like a child's plastic pop-beads. Perhaps the necklace is punctuated by carrot slices—bright orange medallions interspersed among the green orbs.

"Come along; I'll show you."

Our footsteps echo as we walk together over to the chimp necklace, which is enshrined in a large glass case. A messy-looking affair several feet long, it consists, according to the interpretive sign, of the fur and skin of a red colobus monkey from Tanzania. I don't see any trace of vegetable matter. The hide has mostly been reduced to a sturdy string that joins four narrow strips of reddish-brown fur. Oddly, one end is fastened to the middle in an actual knot, possibly tied "accidentally" by the chimp, giving it more the appearance of a necktie than a necklace—but who am I to argue with the ethologists here?

This item raises many questions, most obviously, *Can a chimpanzee tie a knot?* Also, *How was the hide manipulated into this particular, string-like form? What happened to the rest of the red colobus monkey? And where are the vegetables?*

"Where did the chimp get the necklace?"

"We don't know whether she made it or found it, but a wild chimp was wearing the necklace when our scientists first saw her in the jungle. It's the only known example of a chimpanzee necklace."

I'm amazed at how easily William navigates these disparate topics: From the witch in a bottle to recycled items, and now on to this surprising sartorial similarity between chimps and humans. He has taken a step closer to me, inching into my personal space, and his demeanor has changed. William now has the hurried-but-authoritative manner of a man who does not intend to stop talking for a very long time.

Together, we view a black mask with large white teeth and red lips and eyes. It's a demon-mask from Sri Lanka, purchased by the museum in 1893. "It causes shivering fits," William explains. Nearby, a painted mask collected in 1958 depicts the elaborate horned coiffures worn by Annang Ibibio women on special occasions, "particularly when they emerged from their period of seclusion in the *fattening houses* where they were prepared for marriage." An opalescent pink Noh mask with golden teeth and eyes sprouts two slender horns. "This one represents a hannya, the spirit of a beautiful woman transformed through jealousy into a revenge-seeking demon," William says. "See the hair painted onto the forehead of the one next to it? That represents an older or mentally disturbed woman."

This last one induces my own shivering fit. I decide

I will be more comfortable exploring alone, and begin to back away. William takes a moment to return the hankie to his pocket, and I complete my escape, retreating into the museum's gothic darkness.

On to new mysteries, I discover a case of *Amulets, Cures and Charms*: dried seahorses, mermaid necklaces, strings of cowrie shells. These are my favorites. They conjure up the possibilities of transformative magic, like the *akua'ba* doll from Ghana, used to ensure female fertility, a carved bone wand used by a Haida doctor, a boar's tusk pulled by a shaman from the knee of a rheumatic Indian man.

In the midst of all these mesmerizing curiosities, in a case labeled *Magic and Trial by Ordeal*, I spy an antique glass bottle, about three inches long. Silvered from the inside, it is opaque. This bottle has the voluptuous hourglass-like shape of a gourd—or a woman—smaller on the top, larger on the bottom, and reminds me of an expensive perfume container, except that it's stoppered with what looks like an old cigar stub. A yellowed label authenticating its provenance is written in a spidery scrawl:

> Obtained about 1915 from an old lady living in a village near Hove, Sussex. She remarked "... and they do say there be a witch in it, and if you let un out there it be a peck o' trouble."

Voila! I have found the witch in a bottle! She has apparently been consigned to dwell eternally in this little glass vessel. I watch closely for a few seconds, waiting for a flicker of movement inside, listening for the muffled cry of an enraged banshee. But there is no sign of life.

Perhaps she's napping. I tap a little code on the glass case with my fingernails: *Briiip, briiip, briiip-rip-rip.* Nothing. Certainly nothing that seems like it could cause a "peck o' trouble."

What kind *o' trouble?* I wonder. *Was there a mix-up with the magic potions? Did a broomstick fly out of control? Perhaps someone's plump little children were eaten? Also, how did the woman who donated the bottle know about the witch? Had she herself been subjected to objectionable spells or curses, and if so, what had she done to deserve such drastic treatment? Who actually put the witch into the bottle, and how were they able to lure her into containment?*

As I ponder the witch and her unknowable transgressions, I begin to recognize a continuity in the museum's exhibits, and what William was trying to explain. Illness and infertility, unhappiness with our bodies, fear of people unlike ourselves—humans all around the world, over the ages, have had the same sorts of problems. This collection of solutions shows our similarities, our differences, and, sometimes, remarkably inventive remedies—like the witch in a bottle, which strikes me as quite a resourceful method of subduing an annoying sorceress.

I peer into the case again. *One hundred years,* I think, *is an awfully long time to have been locked away. Eternity is even longer.* I begin to feel some sympathy for the witch.

Maybe I should break her out!

William is nowhere in sight. Surreptitiously, I check the integrity of the case. Its lock holds. The frail oak framing would be easy enough to split, and the glass panes are surprisingly thin. I imagine the tinkling sound they would make if they broke. I also imagine the consequences of being caught destroying property at the Pitt Rivers Museum. I would be in a peck o' trouble myself.

Perhaps I should reconsider. The bottle lies silently in its case. *It's possible the witch has already escaped. Are they absolutely sure she is still inside? If she is, and I free her, there will be no way to put all that trouble back into the bottle.* In the end, I am unwilling to risk my own incarceration to liberate the mysterious sorceress. She'll have to remain in her shapely silver bottle, luring visitors to the museum long after we've forgotten Harry Potter.

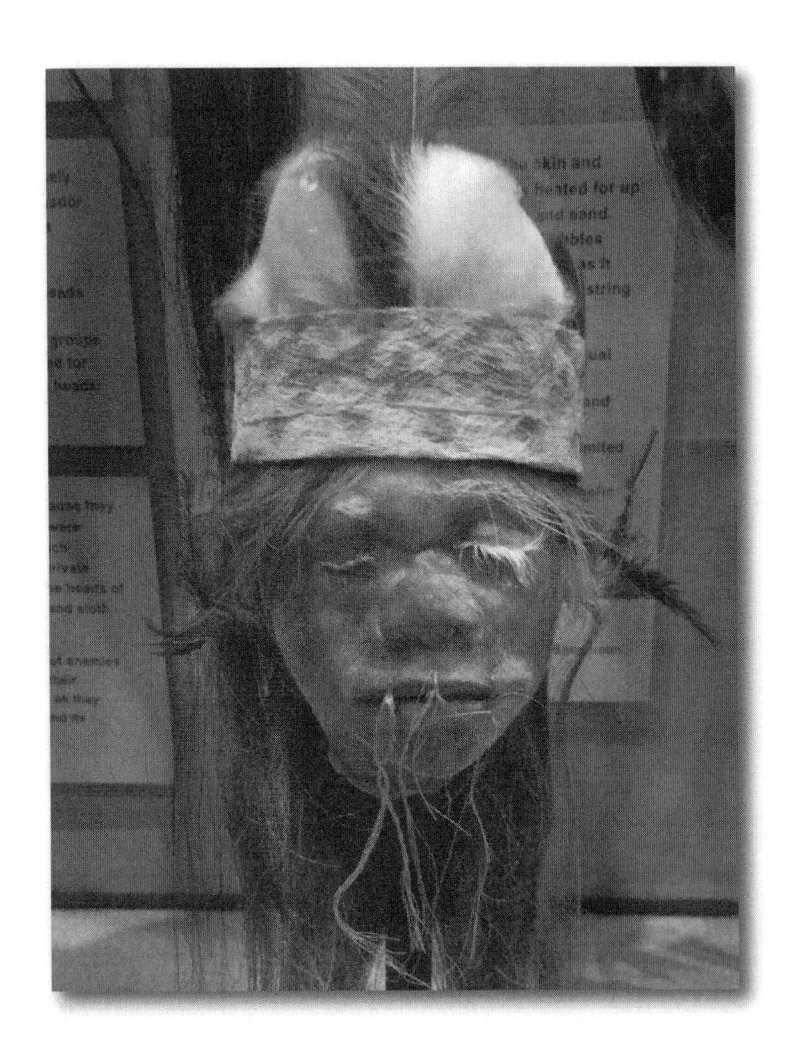

The Treatment of Dead Enemies

Keep your head about you ...

Four decapitated heads, each the size of a large grapefruit, materialize as my eyes adjust to the shadows. The heads, which hang at eye level on thin cords, each have long dark hair and shiny black faces, with eyes and lips that are sutured shut. They are human heads, on display in a tall glass case at the Pitt Rivers Museum in Oxford, England.

I creep forward until my nose touches the glass, and gawk. Two of the heads sport long, braided hair with red and white feathers plaited in, and decorative threads sewn into their upper and lower lips. The other two look more natural, with straight hair and no facial adornments. They are *tsantsas*—shrunken heads—made by the Shuar and Achuar people who live in the Amazonian rainforest.

We—the tsantsas and I—share a cavernous room,

three stories high and crowded with display cases set at cockeyed angles to form an incomprehensible maze. To my right is a wall populated with tribal masks from around the world: Nigeria, Sri Lanka, India, Japan. The Japanese Noh theater masks are particularly beautiful, with their clean lines, subtle coloration, and remarkably evocative expressions of a whole range of emotions, from serene joy to pain and terror.

I feel a faint bit of terror myself, as I wander through the exhibit called *Treatment of Dead Enemies*. It contains examples of human remains and associated objects from around the world—including the four tsantsas. I study the tsantsas, struck by the realization that they once belonged to individual human beings, each with their own unique faces. One of the shrunken visages features high, broad cheekbones, a straight nose, and a pronounced lower jawline. Another is still graced by a long, sloping forehead and an oddly dainty nose.

A small sign in the display case explains:

> In many countries, including our own, the taking of heads from enemies was a socially approved form of violence with deep religious and cultural meanings. It was not seen simply as murder, but as a way of maintaining social order. In England, as shown by the print on display, heads of executed traitors were at one time displayed to deter others from such crimes.

That phrase, "as shown by the print on display," is telling. The museum has been criticized as a bizarre freak show that misrepresents and disrespects the more aggressive behaviors of other cultures. The staff have given a lot of thought to the ethical issues and inequities involved in displaying human remains, and have positioned an illustration of the impaled heads of Guy Fawkes and his co-conspirators (infamous for their traitorous role in the British Gunpowder Plot of 1605) next to the tsantsas, thus pointing out the similarities between the two as an acknowledgment that even the proper English have, in the distant past, beheaded their enemies.

A portly, silver-haired woman approaches the *Treatment of Dead Enemies* display and stands beside me, gazing at the heads. She wears a floral shirtwaist dress and sensible shoes.

After observing the tsantsas for a moment, she says, "One of these was used in the Harry Potter film, *The Prisoner of Azkaban.* Do you know the story of the shrunken heads?"

"Not really," I reply, suspecting I may be about to find out.

The woman clears her throat. "Beginning late in the nineteenth century, the heads were discovered by European explorers and became popular collectibles. They ended up in world-class museums like the

Smithsonian, the Branly in Paris, and the Ethnographic Museum in Berlin. I've seen them all."

She seems very proud of this. "You've seen shrunken heads all around the world?" I ask.

"Yes, I rather like them."

"Really? Why?"

"They tell a story, a human story, just like your American Hatfields and McCoys. The Shuar and Achuar—the two head-shrinking tribes—were similar in many ways, but they fought each other fiercely for ages."

"Probably disputes over land ..." I speculate.

"No, no!" The elderly lady waggles her plump right forefinger in the air like a school marm. "They were avenging the deaths of relatives killed in previous clashes. They were worried that the spirits of their ancestors would return from the netherworld, angry and seeking retribution for their own deaths, and cause havoc for the tribe."

"I see the problem. It's a vicious cycle."

"Yes, the worst kind. You see, they were more afraid of their ancestors' spirits than they were of dying on the battlefield. Bringing back the trophy head appeased the ancestors."

"So what happened after the trophy hunters got the heads?"

"They skedaddled home, of course."

"I guess I'd do the same, under the circumstances," I reply, imagining what it would be like to live in a society that held onto grudges for generations. Our escalating tendencies toward wall-building and polarized politics are giving me the feeling I already live in just such a place. I've dreamed of relocating, but am not really sure where I could go to escape acrimony and friction. They seem to be everywhere.

"Then there were the ceremonies," the lady continues. Her voice is surprisingly low. If I hadn't been looking at her I'd have thought I was talking to David Attenborough.

"What kind of ceremonies did they have?"

"It was a complex process involving feasts for the trophy-hunter's entire clan—the schedule could stretch to a year or more. It was crucial to take specific precautions to subdue the enemy's soul and protect the killers from spiritual revenge."

"Hence the shrinking?"

"Yes, the shrinking and the ceremonies."

"How did they ... um ... how did they do it?"

"It's a bit gruesome," elderly Ms. Attenborough chuckles. "First, the flesh was peeled away from the skull." She glances directly into my eyes to see how I am taking this, perhaps trying to decide how much detail to disclose.

"That sounds difficult," I observe, fascinated and

therefore silently vowing to show no sign of revulsion. I want to find out what she knows.

"Well, after the *fftttt...*" she slices her left hand surreptitiously through the air at neck level to indicate decapitation ... "they made an incision up the back of the head, and separated the skin from the skull. Then they discarded the brains, sewed the eyes and mouth closed, and put the head into a pot of boiling water, with herbs to help preserve the skin."

"They *boiled* the heads?" Somehow, this does not sound right. I envision potatoes bobbing in a pot of boiling water.

"Well, more likely they were simmered for a couple of hours. The timing was critical: not enough and the skin wouldn't come off neatly." She apparently knew the recipe in surprising detail. Questions crowded my own head: *Why didn't the skin end up all wrinkly like mine does after a long bath? How many experiments had it taken to arrive at this precise procedure? And how did this woman know so much about shrunken heads anyway?*

"Do you think they ever overcooked them?" I prodded.

"That was an issue, too. Too long in the pot and the hair would fall out."

"What kind of herbs did they use?" I'm thinking of parsley ... to go with the potatoes.

"Something with tannins. They also used hot sand and rocks to shape the head and preserve the skin, which eventually turned dark and rubbery."

"And that was it?"

"There was one more step—the most important," this sweet granny says, drawing out the suspense. I get the feeling she might be playing me. "The headhunter rubbed charcoal on the skin to seal it and keep the avenging spirit from seeping out."

"That's a clever finale. But why would the Amazonians sell the heads after all that work—especially to foreigners?"

"They didn't really care about the heads themselves. It was the spirit contained in the head—the deceased man's soul—that was important."

"But if the spirit was inside the head, wouldn't they need to hold onto the head itself...?"

"Actually, no. At the end of the ceremonies, the soul would have been expelled from the tsantsa, rendering the trophy quite useless. That's why they were so readily traded."

"Right. Who wants a used shrunken head hanging around the house...?"

"Exactly." She chuckles again and turns to smile broadly at me. I wonder how many times she has told this story, and how her other various audiences have reacted. "Towards the turn of the century the Shuar began trading the heads for guns, which let them kill more Achuar, producing more heads. They became quite popular collectibles."

"So these would mostly be Achuar heads?"

"Perhaps. They might be counterfeits. You have to be very careful about what you're getting."

"Counterfeit heads?" I peer into the case more closely, leaving a foggy little cloud on the glass. It dissipates quickly, then reappears with each exhale.

"Yes. They were so popular with foreigners that counterfeits made from sloth or monkey heads became common—the Amazonians believe humans were descended from sloths. They're actually quite hard to tell from human heads, after all the processing. Many of the counterfeits ended up in museums, too."

"What do you think about these?"

"Take a close look at the ears," she instructs, without bothering to look for herself. "They retain their shape during the shrinking process, so the real thing has miniature human ears."

These look real to me, but I don't have a basis for comparison because I have never actually examined a sloth's ear.

"One can also check for nasal hairs," she continues. "Non-human specimens don't have them."

It's been a fascinating conversation, but I'm beginning to wonder about this lady's mastery of the details.

The Amazonian people wouldn't have had much body hair, and the boiling surely would have compromised it. So the presence of nasal hair doesn't seem like it would be a reliable indicator. For all I know, she's making this stuff up.

Mrs. A goes on to talk about Guy Fawkes, capital punishment ("from the Latin *capitis*, or *head*"), and the practice of decapitation ("It stretches back to Roman times, you know"). Apparently the ancient Celts did it; so did the Chinese and Koreans, and it continues in present-day Saudi Arabia, where it's referred to as "judicial decapitation."

"That's quite a history!" I finally say.

"Yes, it's the history of humankind. Every culture needs to maintain social order. And every culture has traditions that seem illogical—or even superstitious—to outsiders."

At this point I can't help but recollect other part-preserving exhibits I've visited: pickled fetuses in Russia, Louis the XIV's heart resting in a baroque seventeenth-century Parisian cathedral. I've heard that Galileo's middle finger is enshrined in an egg-shaped glass reliquary at a museum in Florence, and that Thomas Edison's last breath, or perhaps a few molecules of it, is on invisible display in a test tube at the Henry Ford Museum in Dearborne, Michigan. The urge to preserve is universal.

But why do shrunken heads seem so much more significant than, say, hair or fingernail clippings, even though they're all body parts? Is it possible there is something remaining in those *memento mori*, some miraculous agency that connects us with a spirit world?

And why is a sweet little old lady so fascinated with the tsantsas? Why are entire exhibits devoted to the likes of Guy Fawkes and other symbols of revenge? I suppose some part of human nature will always be preoccupied with death, enemies and yes, even spirits in shrunken heads. But how much better is it to encounter this fascination here, in a museum ... and not on a neighbor's fence post.

Portal to the Uncanny Valley

Laffing Sal requests your presence

Charmed from afar by San Francisco's reputation for wild eccentricity, I moved there from Iowa right out of college. I wanted to dive into the city's legendary counter-culture: to poke around the dusty remnants of beat writers at City Lights bookstore, take newly available classes in wholistic healing out in the Sunset District, attend political rallies, undertake artistic and spiritual pursuits, explore whatever was left of the Haight and its hippies ... maybe even meet Grace Slick or Jerry Garcia. San Francisco did not disappoint then, and now—decades later—my adopted home still delivers.

I especially love to wander along the waterfront, a circus of sailing ships and fresh seafood, kitsch and kayakers, clanging cable cars and the huge, embarrassingly phallic Coit Tower. What a city! When

I discovered that Suzie, my good friend and fellow travel writer, shared my fascinations we decided to develop a guide-to-the-waterfront mobile app, and spent many happy hours exploring San Francisco's attractions. We made a good team; Suzie was especially knowledgeable about the historical sites, and I had a nose for weirdness.

Some days we'd start out at Ocean Beach, where the Camera Obscura perches on a precipice. Inside the camera housing, mirrors and lenses project live images onto dark walls. Seal Rock, the Cliff House, and Sutro Cliffs appear in muted colors, rotate slowly, then fade into the obscurity of a steady surf, mesmerizing anyone who ventures into the intimate space. "There's an eye on top of the pyramid," says Robert Tacchetto, who has operated the Camera Obscura since 1995. "That's the symbol of the cosmic eye, seeing everything. Well, that's my interpretation."

We'd head in to Baker Beach, birthplace of the iconic Burning Man, and then over to the Presidio, with its Yoda fountain and the military Pet Cemetery, a half-acre of love surrounded by a white picket fence. There are memorials to Poochie and Sheesa and a yellow canary named Sweet Alyssum, nestled, appropriately, in an overgrown patch of blossoming sweet alyssum.

"Four hundred twenty-four tiny tombstones, all for

animals." Suzie observed. "What do you think—creepy or sweet?"

"Um, 'Here lies Pudgy. The best pigeon ever.' That's sweet."

"I say creepy. Here's a monument to someone's dead lizard, 'Mr. Iguana.' They didn't even bother to name him." Suzie leaned in for a closer look.

"I had a horned toad that I never named, when I was a kid. I flushed it when it died. In retrospect, I think it might have just been hibernating."

"You should have buried it. Maybe it would've come back to life in the spring."

"Not after an Iowa winter."

"Good thing you're in California now."

On the way in to Fisherman's Wharf sits the mysterious Wave Organ, a surf-activated acoustic sculpture at the end of a claw-shaped jetty reaching into the Bay. A tenuous production not quite on land, but not completely in the sea, the Wave Organ is an assemblage of carved granite and marble chunks rescued from a demolished cemetery, plus twenty-five bizarre "organ pipes" made of cement and PVC—all held together with concrete and brickwork. You have to listen with an unhurried ear to hear the subtle music produced by waves sloshing into the pipes at high tide. That's where we came up with the idea of a self-guided Quirk-O-Rama Quest, "Because you're not in Kansas anymore, Laurie."

"Iowa is not Kansas," I objected.

"I know, but think about it; how could you be any farther from your midwestern roots? You're sitting on the edge of the world, listening to music *from the ocean* that changes from season to season, from high tide to low. It's so beautiful here!"

"And pretty trippy."

Other days we'd begin on the Embarcadero at the Exploratorium, "Where the right answer is a question." Often called the world's best science museum, it's filled with hands-on experiments that have you touching a tornado, breaking light apart, or listening with your bones. The pitch-dark Tactile Dome is a favorite of locals. Inside, you can walk, crawl, and climb led only by your sense of touch—if you dare; it's scarier than it sounds.

Sometimes we'd hang out at Fort Mason Center, stopping in at the Long Now Foundation where we'd marvel at the idea of a clock designed to tick for 10,000 years—about the age of civilization itself.

"You know Brian Eno composed a melody-generator for clock's chimes," Suzie said.

"The musician?"

"Yeah; he's the one who came up with the name, too: The Long Now."

"I'm kind of embarrassed to admit that the Long Now blows my mind. I can't even begin to think that far into the future."

"I don't think anyone can stretch their imagination that much," Suzie says. "But Eno thought it was important to try. He called its opposite, the Short Now, 'our peculiar form of selfishness, a studied disregard of the future.'"

"What if we could ...?" I ventured.

"We'd take better care of the Earth, that's for sure. It's like the Native Americans' idea of taking into account the next seven generations when making a decision."

"Let's see, about four generations in one hundred years makes four hundred generations in ten thousand years. Nope, I definitely can't think that far into the future."

We'd stop in at the Magic Theater ("Price of Admission: Your Mind"), and gape at Aquatic Park Cove, where human "polar bears" swim 40 miles or more in the frigid San Francisco Bay every winter.

A couple of blocks down the street is the Wax Museum at Fisherman's Wharf, with its nearly three hundred figures constructed to exacting specifications using medical-quality glass eyeballs, porcelain teeth, and human hairs inserted into the scalp one strand at a time with a special needle. Both of us were repulsed by the place so we never went in, but we heard it had a wonderfully gruesome Chamber of Horrors and the world's only wax tableaux recreation of King Tut's

Tomb. The most popular part of the wax museum is apparently its Gallery of Stars, with eerie likenesses of Humphrey Bogart, Marilyn Monroe and Mariah Carey, who actually looks pretty strange to me in real life, with those preternaturally perky cheeks.

Across the street is my favorite spot. Beloved by San Franciscans for its quirky charm, Musée Mécanique is a dimly lit museum housing more than 300 antique contraptions stockpiled by a man named Ed Zelinsky. Zelinsky started collecting when he was eleven—in 1933—beginning with a skill game he bought for five cents and used to extract money, mostly from his friends and family, to purchase penny arcade games. The best part is, you can actually play the antiques that are on display here, although these days you need a roll of quarters. Zelinsky's coin-operated mechanical musical instruments, peep shows, and music boxes sit next to miniature animated dioramas of a circus, a band of seven monkey musicians, and several barely-moving wooly mammoths. For just twenty-five cents you can get your fortune told by the Gypsy Card Reader or have your palm read by sticking it into a scary black hole that forms the mouth of the Bocca della Veritas (the Mouth of Truth). Try out the Kiss-O-Meter ("Measure the Thrill of Your Kisses") or arm wrestle with a legless, red-masked, almost life-sized creature that looks like a love child of The Hulk and Spiderman.

Musée Mécanique's most famous character is ninety-year-old Laffing Sal, a six-foot-tall, clown-like automaton who is famous for terrifying little children. She will either creep you out or annoy you with her gap-toothed smile and raucous laughter. (And perhaps with the spelling of her name, as well.)

"Did you know Laffing Sal is a portal to the Uncanny Valley?" I began as we entered the museum one crisp autumn morning. Laffing Sal, who stands in a booth just inside the front door, towered over us.

"What's the Uncanny Valley?"

"I hoped you'd ask. It's a psychological concept I read about. It's mostly used by robot designers and CGI artists in movies, and basically says we feel an affinity to things that look human—the more human they look, the more we connect with them—until they reach a stage where they're almost, but not quite, realistic. Then we get creeped out. That's the Uncanny Valley."

"Makes sense, I guess. I get the "uncanny" part, but what about the valley?"

"That's because the inventor of the concept drew a graph to illustrate it. The horizontal axis..."

"Is that the x or the y axis? I can never remember."

"Me neither. Anyway, the sideways axis represents how human a thing looks, and the vertical axis represents how much affinity or affection we feel

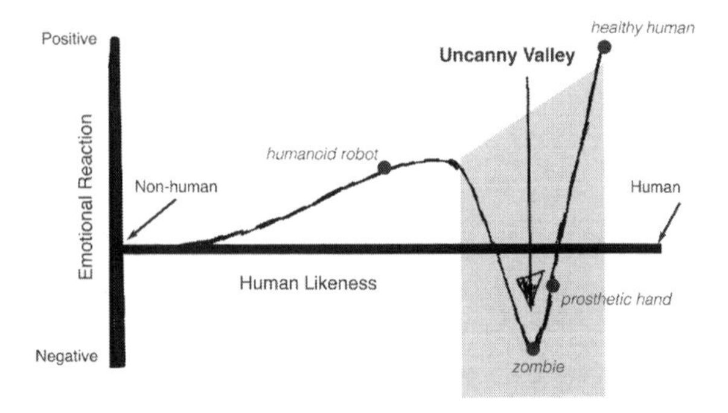

toward the thing. The graph line starts going up from bottom left to top right, but then at that Uncanny Valley stage, where something looks almost-but-not-quite human, there's this big dip—that's the valley."

"Where things get creepy," Suzie says. "Like Laffing Sal, or clowns. Oh—that's probably why we hate the wax museum, too."

"Right. One of several reasons. I've been researching the Uncanny Valley, and I found some great stuff. Do you want to get really creeped out?" As usual, I want to take the concept one step further: how and why the Uncanny Valley reaction may be preprogrammed into us; the probable role of mirror neurons in the reaction; the whole issue of "H+" human beings with enhanced characteristics.

"Right now?" Suzie is busy depositing a quarter into the "English Execution" exhibit. We watch, entranced, as two tiny castle doors swing open, revealing a gallows inside. We've only just glimpsed a miniature man with a noose around his neck when the floor beneath him slides open and the figure is hanged. It is both horrible and delightful.

"Google 'teddy bear with dentures,'" I suggest.

Suzie opens her phone and pulls up multiple images of teddy bears with dentures. Apparently it's a thing. They are surprisingly unnerving. "Yep, that's *definitely* creepy. It would be right at home here, next to the musical monkey band."

"Isn't it amazing? They don't even need to look human to evoke the Uncanny Valley. OK, now pull up 'Real Life Barbie.'"

Suzie doesn't yet share my fascination with this particular weirdness, but she thumbs the words into her phone. "Valeria Lukyanova?"

"That sounds right; check her out."

"Oh my god—is that a real person? She actually *does* look like a Barbie doll."

A *GQ* article from 2017 shows a photo of "Barbie" at the beach. A first look gives the impression that this is a plastic Barbie doll posed on a sandy beach, but the headline insists it is an actual human being. "Meeting Valeria Lukyanova," says author Michael Idov, "is the closest you will come to an alien encounter ... A living Barbie is automatically an Uncanny Valley Girl."

I have researched this, too. If Barbie—the doll—

were a real woman, she'd be 5'9" tall and weigh 110 pounds—definitely anorexic. Her freakishly buoyant bustline would measure 39" and she'd wear a size three shoe. She'd also have room for only half a liver and a few inches of intestine, and would be so top-heavy she'd need to walk on all fours, especially if she insisted on wearing high heels.

Suzie and I move on to another exhibit—a nameless papier-mâché man dressed in a P.T. Barnum-like circus barker costume. He could definitely be Laffing Sal's brother. The man holds his overcoat open, flasher-style, to reveal a sign reading: *ANTIQUES Sold for Reasonable PRICES.*

There is something troubling about that placard. More than the irrationally exuberant capitalization, more than the ironic *meta*-ness of an antique advertising the sale of antiques, there is something unsaid, something implied and unsettling. It reminds me of the sign at the Magic Theater: *Price of Admission: Your Mind.*

The man holding the sign has a huge bald head with eyeballs that move creepily from side to side, and eyebrows that rise and fall slowly ... reluctantly ... hypnotically ...

I believe we have reached the portal.
Today will be a fine day to explore
the Uncanny Valley.

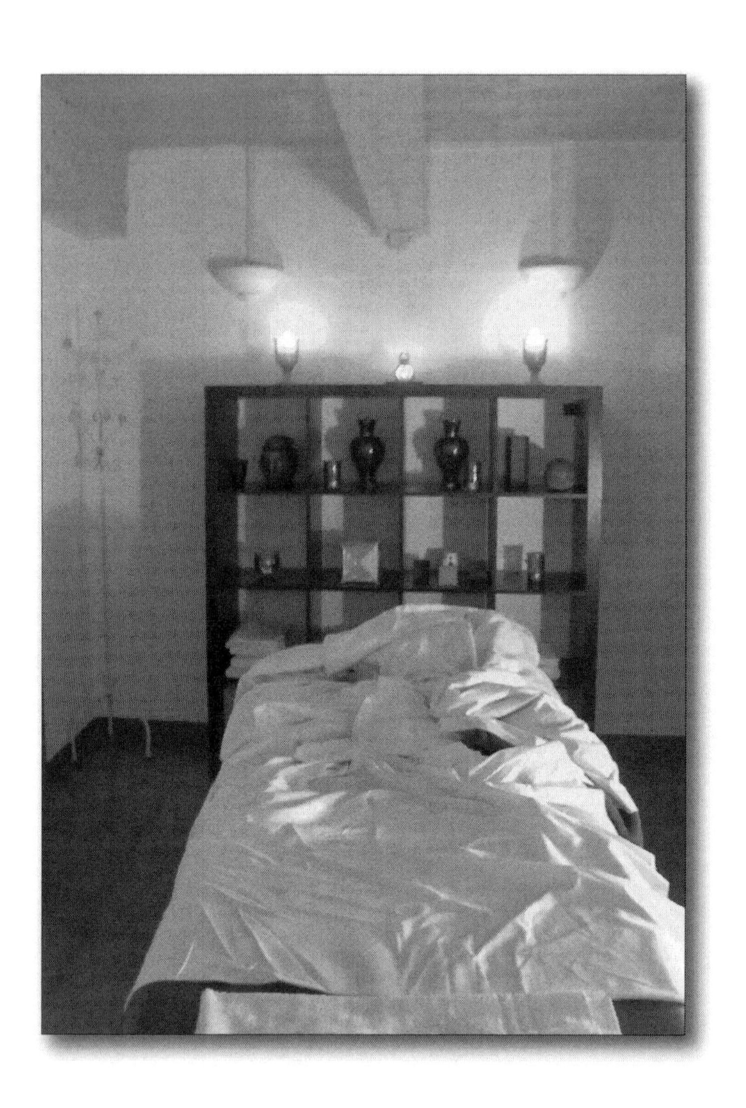

Tears and Tiramisu

Italian spirits raise existential questions

"You will cry. You will *definitely* cry." I had just arrived at a secluded retreat center near Orvieto in northern Italy, and plopped onto a pillow-filled couch next to Rebecca, who was also staying there. It had been a tough few years—my parents had died, my employment situation was suboptimal—and I'd booked this trip for a sorely needed vacation. Although we had barely met, Rebecca was already pushing one of the spa services on offer. "Laura's healing massages are awesome!" she enthused. "They will make you cry."

Not likely, I thought, brushing the idea aside. It seemed improbable that a masseuse would make me cry. Rebecca rearranged the pillows and scooched closer to me, her bright red hair bouncing. "You should book one right away," she continued. "Laura's schedule will fill up fast. The meals here are fabulous, too. Don't forget to make reservations for dinner." Rebecca reminded me of Rome's Trevi Fountain, eternally bubbling.

The retreat center, which focused on healing arts like meditation and yoga, reminded me of Old World Italy, too. A pastiche of aging family portraits and gigantic, exuberant floral still lifes in gilded frames warmed the pale stone walls. Fresh lilacs in tall vases, worn oriental rugs, and a baby grand piano crowded the sitting room. The scent of baking bread filtered through a carved wooden screen leading to the kitchen, its aroma beckoning me back to the times of classic works of art and faded antiquities.

It was May—a perfect time to visit this country

villa, its patio trellis draped with sweet-smelling wisteria, the air heady with blossoms and herbs. Rose bushes climbed the front of the building and popped up here and there on the grounds, along with clumps of lavender. In the distance a carefully tended vegetable garden rolled out in long rows that supplied much of the villa's produce; beyond that lay rolling hills covered with vineyards, their new leaves bright in the spring sunshine. Bees buzzed faintly in the distance.

I was not sure Rebecca and I had the same understanding of the words *awesome* or *healing*. I *was* sure I didn't want to cry on vacation, especially during a massage. Did Laura specialize in deep tissue bodywork, performed with such ferocity I'd wail in pain? Would it somehow connect me with a past life in which I was eaten by a lion or poisoned by one of the Borgias' arsenic-laced concoctions? I had misgivings, but massages always seem like a good idea, so I went ahead and booked one.

When massage time came, I entered a small, peaceful room lighted with flickering candles. A dozen tiny bottles of aromatic essences stood on a side table; woodsy incense and meditative music with a distinct whalesong backbeat filled the chamber.

Laura was waiting. Dark, wavy Botticelli tresses framed her face, which was clear and pale. Her cheeks were pink, and she favored red clothing. "Undress to your knickers, or all the way, whatever you're comfortable with," she instructed.

I stripped and hopped onto the table, feeling curious and a bit apprehensive. When would the crying part begin? Laura rubbed massage oil lightly onto my back. "Mmmm, that smells nice," I murmured. It was an enigmatic combination: sharp yet sweet, energizing yet relaxing.

"That's because it's for you. This is what *they* told me to use. It's scented with sweet orange, geranium, and lavender."

They? Uh-oh, I thought. *This is going to be way too New-Agey.* Laura had blended an aromatherapy oil especially for me, as instructed by ... by whatever *beings* she was communicating with. I didn't ask who was providing the information, preferring to relax and enjoy the massage.

"You may experience some strange bodily sensations," Laura whispered. "Or you might feel like laughing or crying; that's OK. Just go with whatever comes up."

It was an odd "massage." Laura's hands floated across my skin. There was no pressure or kneading. And I never felt even a little bit like laughing or crying during the entire hour.

Once, though, when Laura touched the inside of my

left leg, just above the knee, my throat tightened up. Later—I don't remember which body part she was working on—my lips went numb and buzzy. Was this because I was lying face down on the massage table, with my face hanging through the head-hole? My lips are not accustomed to being the lowest part of my body. Perhaps extra blood was flowing into them and pooling there, causing the odd sensation.

That feeling faded and a new one floated in: My upper and lower teeth felt like they had fused together. It was subtle, and lasted only a few seconds.

When the massage was over, Laura asked, "Do you want to know what they told me?"

"Yes, please." Of course I wanted to know what her mysterious messengers had to say! After all, they'd done a good job choosing the massage oil. Who knew what else they would come up with.

"Actually, you are quite OK," Laura said softly.

That's a good way to begin, I thought. *Keep the customer happy.*

"You have been through a lot of trauma in figuring out who you are and what you are here to do," Laura continued, speaking rapidly. "You still feel this and you are right: You *haven't* figured it out."

How could a stranger possibly have discerned that I'd spent years in therapy anguishing over what I should do with my life?

"A man, I think your father, has told you that everything you say is worthless," Laura continued. "That is your trauma."

This was getting eerie. How could Laura have perceived the impossible riddle I was raised with—the one in which Dad taught me to think for myself then disagreed with many of my conclusions?

Let me be clear: I object, in principle, to giving a so-called psychic any information to corroborate her guesses. But Laura was so completely correct on both these points that I *had* to acknowledge it. I nodded ever so slightly, and allowed the tears that had suddenly appeared to slip out the corners of my eyes.

"You have learned to consider very carefully everything you say. You do not spew negativity into the world, as many people do. They do not realize the effect of their words. But you understand how important words are; that is your gift."

"You are here to say something to someone, to help someone with your words. I think it is a boy. What do you do in life?"

"I'm a writer," I began. "I thought maybe my gift might be my stories ..."

"Yes, that may very well be. But it is your *spoken* words that are your real gift."

I didn't mention the strange sensations I'd had in my throat, teeth and lips—all body parts that are essential to the spoken word.

"You and your father may have been on opposite sides in a previous incarnation. Maybe you were the bad one and hurt him. Maybe the two of you decided, *OK, we'll switch it around this time.* It often works that way," she continued. "It will take a few days for you to absorb this information. You may have strange dreams during this time; pay attention to them. We are like babies; they look down and laugh at our attempts. It takes practice; start small, and when you have something to say, say it." And that was the end of the message, as well as the massage.

Which was a good thing, because bodywork makes me hungry, and the tantalizing aromas of citrus and rosemary were drifting into the room. It was dinnertime, and I was ready for a good meal. I dressed in the dim candlelight and floated off to the dining room, choosing a secluded corner table so I could contemplate the messages Laura had relayed. My only companion was a trout that had been baked whole, head and all. It lay before me on a bed of greens, with thin lemon slices layered on top—sunny pinwheels glistening on silver skin. Mounds of couscous and roasted vegetables cozied up to the greens.

I sipped a crisp Orvieto Classico and tried to imagine "them"—whoever that was—looking down on me, laughing. What did Laura mean, *You are here to say something to someone. I think it is a boy*? She was referring to something specific, and to a specific person. Was The Message some hard-earned wisdom? Was there only one sentence, or was it a whole conversation? Would I recognize it when I said it? Maybe I had *already* said it. If so, what did that imply about the remaining years of my life—were they just a meaningless byproduct of the process of getting me in the right place at the right time to say the right thing to the right person?

Digging into the trout seemed like a reasonable response to these complicated questions; after all, my grandmother had always said that fish was brain food. I pushed the skin aside in favor of the delicate meat. It was light and flaky, a little nutty and almost sweet. I squeezed on some lemon juice and licked my fingers, imagining the trout bursting with nutrients that would help me understand this odd experience.

What kind of result was so important that I was put on earth to contribute to it? And if I hadn't already transmitted the message, did I already know it, or should I be studying up, perhaps finding some scholars to converse with? It seemed like quite a responsibility—was I up to the task? Perhaps after another glass of wine.

I started in on the couscous next. It popped in my mouth like caviar; then the vegetables took over: sweet spring peas and fruity chunks of red pepper ... crunchy carrots ... onions, celery, zucchini, three kinds of beans.

I moved on to the smoky eggplant, roasted with cherry tomatoes and garnished with walnut halves and fresh basil.

Maybe I was making The Message into too big a deal. Perhaps it could be prosaic—something like *Your classroom is down the hall on the left*—because it was just one humble step on the way to some final result far in the future. The boy would go on to develop a robust unified field theory, or eradicate disease or ensure world peace. My words would be part of an intricate jigsaw puzzle, the pieces all slipping together into an elegant, preordained outcome. But wait ... if the outcome were preordained, wouldn't that mean there was no such thing as free will?

At this point I began to worry that my head might explode, so I started in on dessert—a classic tiramisu. My fork slipped through a cloud of zabaglione, mascarpone, and whipped cream, then dipped into the ladyfingers softened in espresso. That first bite was so smooth and cool I no longer cared whether my life had any meaning. Nor did I care about The Message, the boy, or the problem of free will. In that moment, the pure pleasures of earthly existence—the massage oil lingering on my skin, the wine, which had gone to my head, the delicious meal and the scent of wisteria in a purple twilight—all conspired to open up my senses and get me out of my head.

"So how was the massage?" Rebecca asked, pulling up a chair to join me for dessert. "Did you cry?"

Well yes, I had; the experience with Laura opened up past wounds I hadn't even been aware of. But her acknowledgment of that old pain helped to heal it. And my mood lifted immeasurably as soon as I ate the local trout, swigged a bit of Orvieto Classico, and gorged on dessert. I flashed a Mona Lisa smile at Rebecca and reveled in the last creamy bite of tiramisu. This was surely Italy at its finest.

Into the Kaleidoscope

A Short Walk on a Man-Eating Lake

Be careful where you step

On a small, faraway island lies a lake that devours all things offered to it—and some that are not. In 1998 a young man was hitched to a tractor and towed, with great difficulty, out of the sticky, quicksand-like grip of the Great Pitch Lake on the southern part of the Caribbean island of Trinidad. The ordeal—a battle between the man's rescuers and the inexorable pull of the lake's ten million tons of slowly circulating pitch—took several exhausting hours. At the end of the day the man was still alive, although quite shaken—and his body, from armpits to toes, was covered with a thick coat of gooey black tar. A photo at the lake's small, tidy museum memorializes the incident. Its caption, awkwardly written in black Sharpie around the edge of the photo, says:

"This is a guy that got sink into the mother of the lake."

I'm visiting the Great Pitch Lake, also called Tierra de Brea, or "Land of Pitch," to learn more about Trinidad by immersing myself in the country's geology and prehistory. Not literally, of course. Not like the man who had to be hauled out with a tractor; I don't want *that* kind of authentic reenactment!

A brochure at the visitor's center says I should always walk with an official tour guide, and mentions that the lake is in constant motion, consuming, eventually, "all that is placed upon it." Tyrell, a tall Trinidadian man in a bright orange La Brea shirt, volunteers to show me around.

The surface is immense, stretching out for nearly 100 acres, and the lake's center is said to be 250 feet deep. Veins extend outward for several miles—sinuous feelers reaching out from this black-hole lagoon. I'm eager to learn about the "mother" or middle of the lake, the part that swallowed that poor fellow in 1998, so that is my first question for Tyrell.

"The 'mother' is the softest, most active part of the lake—it will suck in any careless wanderer," he explains. "You want to avoid it, but you cannot tell which areas are safe just by looking."

Then he begins to pitch the pitch. "This," Tyrell says, extending a long arm and gesturing at the lake, "is the 8th Wonder of the World, a tourist attraction with 20,000 visitors a year. It's the largest and most significant pitch lake in the world, and also an active mine, a major supplier of asphalt to the international market. La Brea has paved streets and airport runways in more than fifty countries, including La Guardia in New York."

I'm not interested in the international asphalt market,

so I tune Tyrell out as we stroll toward what looks like a huge, lumpy parking lot. On the edge of the lake, where the asphalt is cooler, it's a dull gray color, cracked and wrinkled. Here and there the surface bulges, pushing up from below. Grasses and low shrubs poke up around the perimeter, and a surprising abundance of birdlife bedazzles the skies—jewel-like hummingbirds, fluttering sandpipers, silent herons and kingfishers, enormous black vultures.

We walk right out onto the surface of the lake, which squishes like soft tar but doesn't stick to my shoes. A network of fissures creates hundreds of hot tub-sized pools, which are joined by little creeks in a landscape of tiny black islands. There is no particular odor. I'm surprised that no oil slick blankets the water, and that schools of minnows live in the larger pools. That explains the herons and kingfishers.

"See that spot over there?" Tyrell points out over the vast lake. "In the early days of asphalt extraction, a worker drove a tractor out onto the pitch and left it there overnight. The next morning, only the top half remained above the surface, and by noon the tractor was completely gone. The lake will eat anything."

We take a few more steps, Tyrell weaving across the pocked and puckered surface, skirting shallow pools. "In 1928, a massive tree, about 4,000 years old, suddenly arose from the center of the lake, then sank back down. We never saw it again. We never saw the tractor again, either. They're still in there somewhere. *Stay close to me*," he warns.

Tyrell picks up a hefty stick. I follow directly behind him, careful to make my feet land in the exact same places his have just left. The asphalt sinks slightly beneath me with each step and I realize we can't stop moving, or we'll risk sinking. In a few places the skin of the lake is split open, exuding rich black fudge. We are in the middle of a wide expanse of sticky subterranean bitumen, and Tyrell is my only lifeline back to "shore." I am certainly going to stay close behind him. I would probably do anything he asked.

Not everyone is so cautious. As we trek farther onto the lake, I see two families of Trinidadians dressed in swimwear, casually bathing in shallow pools of clear water. This spot is well known for its sulfur-rich waters, which are supposed to cure joint pain and heal skin conditions.

Tyrell tells me about the indigenous Chima people who once lived here. Legend has it that they got so carried away celebrating the defeat of a rival tribe that they cooked and ate a feast of hummingbirds, using the beautiful leftover feathers to decorate themselves.

Hummingbirds, tiny as they are, do not seem to me like the obvious choice for a feast—nor would their teensy feathers go very far in decorating a human body, but perhaps times were tough. At any rate, the decision angered their god, who created the pitch lake to swallow the errant revelers. It was an easy legend to believe, in part because of the many Amerindian artifacts that have been discovered here, preserved for eons in the pitch.

At the museum I'd learned more about the lake, and what it spits up. In addition to the tractor and the prehistoric tree, it has relinquished shards of ancient pottery, a mastodon tooth, and the fossilized thigh bone of a giant sloth.

"This asphalt pit—the world's largest—was created when two continental plates collided," Tyrell continues. "They opened a fault line, which allowed oil to seep up to the earth's surface from deep underground deposits. When the oil came into contact with air, its lighter elements evaporated, leaving the heavy asphalt behind."

Europeans did not hesitate to mine the resource. At the end of the 16th century, the lake was "discovered" by Sir Walter Raleigh, the English adventurer who was in the Americas in search of El Dorado, the legendary Land of Gold. There was enough pitch here, Raleigh calculated, to protect the bottom of the entire British fleet. He caulked his own ships with it in 1595, proclaiming, "It melteth not with the sun as the pitch of Norway." Because of this claim, or perhaps because of Sir Walter Raleigh's special relationship with Queen Elizabeth I, asphalt from the Great Pitch Lake was used to pave a large area in front of Buckingham Palace. Unfortunately, the asphalt *did* melt, miring the royal horses' hooves and carriage wheels with the sticky stuff.

It threatens to do the same thing to my shoes. As Tyrell and I head toward the lake's center, its surface turns stickier, glossier, blacker. We pass a pair of bright orange sandals, half covered in tar and abandoned.

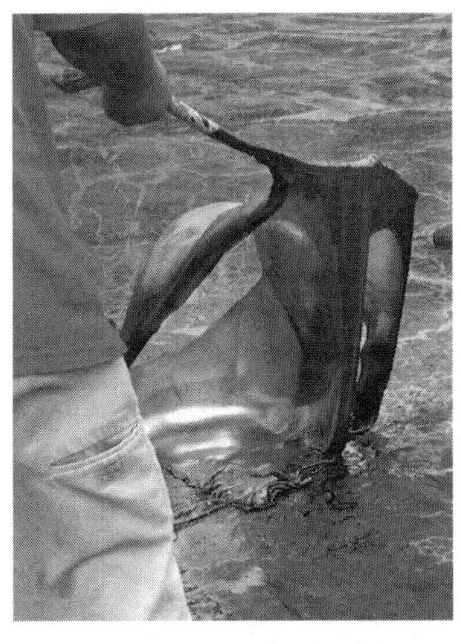

Slowly, the lake comes alive. Motion arises where I do not expect it; water bubbles and gasses hiss as they push to escape its churning depths. Tyrell leans over one particularly shiny spot, dips the stick into the tarry mess, and holds it up; viscous black sheets trail off into thick tendrils, then slip back into the deep well of darkness.

I am mesmerized—entranced. We have entered one of those rare, magical landscapes that transforms before your eyes, revealing its mysteries only after you commit to engaging with it. Pale grasses sway in wind. Their tips are nearly white, but at the base, where they rise from puddles of water, green stems affirm life.

Out on the body of the pitch it is nothing like an

asphalt parking lot. Depth and scale transmute as I slip into an otherworldly landscape. Grasses grow into gorgeous forests, pools morph into lakes, the furrowed grey surface mutates into an elephant's hide. The epidermis moves beneath my feet, shifting ever so slightly, its immeasurable mass giving way to my own weight, challenging my equilibrium. Its ridges and wrinkles emanate a strange beauty and endurance. This landscape—this piercing of the earth's skin—dredges up memories so deep and vague, so primeval and profound I'm not sure they are even mine: fear, danger, motion, inevitability, peace.

As we pick our way back to terra firma, I think: *Tyrell is right. You cannot tell which areas are safe just by looking.* That night I dream I am walking on the man-eating lake and, of course, it is sucking me in. I struggle, but ultimately succumb to the pitch's slow roil, becoming one of the Earth's ancient, organic recollections—recycled, churned to the surface, and swallowed whole again. And then I awaken to the light of day.

Admiral MacBride

Mayflower Memories

The Truth about Tisquantum

"What passes for identity in America is a series of myths about one's heroic ancestors."
—*James Baldwin*

My great-great-great-great-great-great-great-great-great-grandparents, William and Susanna White, immigrated to America on the *Mayflower.* They are heralded as the parents of Peregrine White, born in November, 1620, while the *Mayflower* was still anchored in Cape Cod—and famous as "the first born child of New England," a moniker that conveniently ignored all the indigenous people who had lived here for tens of thousands of years.

I knew little about this background growing up, but

when my grandmother died Dad inherited her papers and became fascinated with the historical documents she'd kept: birth and death records, old newspaper clippings, and family histories that had been handwritten generations ago. He dove into genealogy and eventually constructed a family tree detailing four hundred years' worth of names, dates and relationships, and hung the convoluted illustration on a hallway wall in our house—a constant reminder of our distinguished history.

So when my husband, Jim, and I traveled to England many years later, the first item on my to-do list was visiting the Mayflower Steps—the point of departure for my ancestors who had sailed to North America. There were six: William and Susanna White and their five-year-old son, Resolved (Peregrine's less-celebrated older brother); Sir Francis Cooke, a Leiden Separatist; and the adventurer Steven Hopkins and his wife, Elizabeth.

At first it struck us as odd that so many of my ancestors came to the New World together, but of course that small group would have intermarried. Steven and Elizabeth Hopkins' daughter Damaris, for example, married Sir Francis Cooke's son, Jacob. There was also the fact that many of the 102 *Mayflower* passengers had been religious Separatists back in England, and founding a free colony in the

New World—not to mention populating it with Christ's flock—required dedicated procreation. Some genealogists estimate that today, more than twelve generations later, there are as many as 35 million *Mayflower* descendants.

A friend of ours, Kabba, lives near Plymouth and has generously volunteered to show us around. Kabba is a lean, compact man and an accomplished sailor. He single-handedly captained his twenty-four-foot sailboat across the Atlantic from England to Brazil. Kabba is also witty, educated, and outgoing; he's a wonderful guide.

Driving in to Plymouth, we round a broad curve of grassy lawn and pass Smeaton's Tower, an iconic 72-foot lighthouse banded with five huge red and white stripes that contrast impressively with the cloudless blue sky. We're headed for Sutton Harbor—a surprisingly small working port formerly known as "Sutton Pool"—in a historic, cobblestoned section of town that's now home to theaters, galleries, restaurants, and boutiques. Gulls cry, halyards clang, and the aromas of steak and seafood waft by.

The famous Mayflower Steps lead down from a crowded and unimpressive pier directly into the water. A dozen or so steps are above the surface, depending on the tides. A modest commemorative portico—two

Doric columns flanked by flagpoles—marks their place on the pier. An American flag flies on the right side. A British flag flies on the left.

The steps themselves are pale gray limestone. I sit on the third step from the top, gaze out at boats bobbing in the water, and try to summon the ghosts of my ninth great-grandparents, Stephen and Elizabeth Hopkins, wondering how they felt as they embarked with one hundred other passengers on what would turn out to be a grueling sixty-six days at sea. They would have spent much of their time crouched in cold, wet semi-darkness below the main deck—probably eating salted fish, praying, and heaving with seasickness.

According to his biographer in the book *Here Shall I Die Ashore*, Stephen's adventures began well before the *Mayflower*. He had already been a castaway, sailed to the New World, survived a hurricane in the Bermuda Triangle, and been shipwrecked for nearly a year on the Isle of Devils, "one of the most feared islands of the world." This incident is said to have inspired the shipwreck scene that opens "The Tempest"—Shakespeare's drunken and mutinous character, Stephano, was apparently modeled after my ancestor. Stephen had also attended the marriage of Pocahontas to John Rolfe in Jamestown, and would go on to lodge the famous Squanto in his home.

But this trip was different: the couple had their three children in tow, and Elizabeth was at least six months pregnant with their fourth, Oceanus, one of two babies born onboard the *Mayflower* during the voyage to the New World. The other baby was William and Susanna White's son, Peregrine. Elizabeth and Susanna, along with two other surviving adult women and their daughters, cooked the first Thanksgiving feast the following year.

Stephen Hopkins, William White, and Sir Francis Cooke were among the forty-one men who signed the Mayflower Compact on November 11, 1620—along with better-known Pilgrims such as Captain Myles Standish and John Alden. From sailing across the Atlantic to signing the Mayflower Compact and founding Plymouth Colony, my stalwart ancestors were visionary adventurers with courage, perseverance, and grit. I like to imagine I inherited some of those heroic character traits...

Kabba interrupts my musing. "This isn't really where the *Mayflower* sailed from," he says.

"What do you mean, it isn't? There's a plaque right here memorializing the event." I nod toward a small bronze sign I'd noticed on the wall near the top of the steps.

"What does it actually say?"

I walk over and read it aloud:

> The Honourable Walter Annenberg United States ambassador to the Court of St. James's unveiled this tablet on the 6th September 1970. This day being the 350th anniversary of the sailing of the "Mayflower."

"You see? It only refers to the anniversary. These steps were built in 1934; the steps they actually left from are over there." Kabba tilts his head toward a two-story building a hundred feet away. It's white with a dark brown roof and trim, and an elegantly lettered sign: Admiral MacBride.

"At the Admiral MacBride? A pub?"

"Yeah, that's the place. Things have changed a lot in the last four hundred years. Streets move, buildings come and go. Let's have a look."

We walk over to the Admiral MacBride, which has a long, shiny wooden bar and is decorated with vintage beer posters. The guys order pints.

"So where are the steps?" I ask Kabba.

"Right behind that door." He gestures toward the ladies' loo. "Go check them out."

I walk over to the door. It's locked; I can hear someone inside. I wait. A flush. A woman exits and I enter, dubiously, to find myself in a cramped water closet. Inside is a toilet. Nothing more.

Indignant, I return to the two men, who are now well into their pints.

"Where are the steps, *really*?"

"They're there; the steps are actually there! But you can't see them because they've been built over." I'm not sure why they think that's so hilarious, but Kabba and Jim have a good laugh.

"So much for your illustrious ancestors," Jim teases. "They embarked from a toilet."

"It wasn't a toilet 400 years ago when they left," I protest.

But the guys are just getting started. "And they landed in the wrong place," Jim says.

I do remember, from a history lesson in elementary school, that the *Mayflower* was meant to land in Virginia, but ended up some 500 miles north, in Massachusetts. "They were blown off course," I begin, in the Pilgrims' defense.

"Probably not." Kabba says. Sailors were very good with latitude at that time, and they could easily have sailed on down to Virginia, where the winter would have been milder."

"Why would they have wanted to settle in Virginia, anyway?" Jim asks. "It was controlled by the Anglicans; that's who they were trying to get away from."

"Well, they did sign the Mayflower Compact, which set the stage for self-government in America." I'm trying to rehabilitate the memory of my ancestors, but end up getting into more trouble.

"Didn't you ever read *Lies My Teacher Told Me*?" Jim asks. "The Mayflower Compact isn't the great historical document we've been brainwashed to believe it is. It was a stop-gap to prevent mutiny. Most of the Pilgrims came over because they were poor, and wanted land and money—not because they were burning with the ideals of freedom and democracy. And by the way, the first Thanksgiving origin myth is a hoax."

"You're saying that the first Thanksgiving never happened?"

"I'm saying our idea of it isn't true. What do you think of when you think about Thanksgiving?"

"The Pilgrims and Indians got together and had a feast, and the Pilgrims gave thanks to God for their good fortune."

"And your great-great grannies, who came over on the *Mayflower,* cooked the feast?" Kabba asked, finishing his pint.

"Well, the *men* probably didn't cook it."

"It was the Indians who provided the venison and taught the Pilgrims how to farm and catch fish. Without them, your ancestors would've starved to death. The Pilgrims should have been giving thanks to the Indians."

Back at home, I look up these "new" facts. Squanto

is the biggest surprise. His real name was Tisquantum —apparently shortened to Squanto so young children of future generations could pronounce it in holiday revues. I vaguely remember Squanto as a Native American (well, I remember him as an Indian; that was the term we used then) who knew some English and helped the settlers. What I didn't realize is how he learned the language: he was kidnapped by English explorers, probably in 1614, taken to Spain, and sold as a slave. He lived in Spain and England for several years before returning to North America to help the English "settle"—some historians now use the term "invade"—the new continent.

Squanto was not only a translator; he was an ambassador, a guide, a technical advisor, a fishing instructor, and a farm manager who taught the newcomers to raise corn and squash. What's more, the Pilgrims' settlement at Plymouth was made much easier because the place—once Tisquantum's hometown—had recently been decimated by a plague, leaving a good-sized village with no living inhabitants. As for Thanksgiving, Native Americans had observed fall harvest celebrations for centuries; they may well have introduced the idea to the Pilgrims.

I'm both startled and disappointed to learn all this—that the "history" I was taught in school was such a distortion of the truth, that my teachers didn't prove to be trustworthy, that my ancestors were not the indomitable heroes I had imagined, that we have denigrated the culture and roles of Native Americans so much more than I had realized. To what end?

Best case, revisionist history gives people like me an inspiring origin story: Our ancestors braved untold hardships to create a new, free country. They developed the basis for our legal system, built towns and roads, and did pretty much everything else necessary to bring forth this hallowed nation.

The price of that story, of course, is betrayal. We betrayed the truth. We betrayed the great Native American nation. And by rejecting our own myriad imperfections, we betrayed ourselves. It will take a lot of work to make things right, but here's a place to begin. We can tell the truth, celebrating the contributions of people of color, women, and all the other groups long ignored by our "official" national narrative. We can rewrite history again, one story at a time.

Park of the Fallen Heroes

Where Soviet skeletons come out of the closet

Josef Stalin looms above me. More than ten feet tall, the fearsome ruler stands at ease, his right arm bent at the elbow, hand slipped into his vest beneath a massive pink-granite overcoat. His hair poufs up and back, nicely coiffed. His mustache—smooth, thick and luxurious—contrasts with a rough surface just above it, where Stalin's nose has been smashed off. The right leg was broken and repaired. A tidy green lawn surrounds the statue.

Arcing behind Stalin is a curving concrete-and-metal-bar cage, perhaps forty feet wide and ten feet tall, filled with more than two hundred slightly-larger-than-life-sized heads sculpted from granite. Most are representational but crude, not meant to depict the actual head of any individual human being. They are metaphoric heads, piled six-high into a forty-foot metaphoric prison, staring silently out at all who pass. Rows of barbed wire and gulag-like lamps—poignant symbols of Soviet repression—run neatly along the top of the curving stacks of heads. The effect is chilling. This wrenching memorial is named for and dedicated to "Victims of Soviet-Era Prison Camps"—including the camps run by Stalin, notorious for his purges and the "reforms" that left millions of people dead in the 1930s.

The odd juxtaposition—Stalin and the imprisoned heads—stands at the heart of Moscow's Park of the Fallen Heroes, a sculpture park established in 1992 after the Soviet Union collapsed. Protestors in

Moscow had toppled statues of former Soviet leaders, mutilating some, defacing others, and pushing many into the Moskva River. Later, the fallen monuments were retrieved and dumped *en masse* into a "graveyard" near Gorky Park, where they sat, unattended, for a year.

Someone in the park administration saw an opportunity and created the Park of the Fallen Heroes—an attempt to salvage teachable moments from the riots and vandalization that had ravaged the city. The heads-in-a-cage installation was donated by sculptor Evgeny Chubarov on the condition that it be positioned next to Stalin. A favorite of photographers, the strange memorial is now portrayed on posters available in the United States. You can buy one online at Sears, Walmart, or Amazon.com.

The Park of the Fallen Heroes is home to more than 700 other statues and pieces of sculpture, and they aren't all political: Voluptuous white marble women pose acrobatically in front of a flower bed, bronze lovers caress on freshly clipped grass, a red-white-and-blue wooden Pinocchio relaxes on a bench. The sylvan setting and art-for-art's-sake help defuse the political monuments' original messages.

But the park's purposes are clear. Many memorials depict Lenin. Marx and Brezhnev stand tall, too, along with a fifteen-ton iron monument to Felix

Dzerzhinsky, the infamous first director of the All-Russia Extraordinary Commission to Combat Counter-revolution and Sabotage—which would become the KGB. In August, 1991, Russian protestors crowded Lubyanka Square, where the memorial to Dzerzhinsky dominated its position near KGB headquarters. They demolished the monument with a crane. Broadcast on TV around the world, the event quickly became a symbol of the revolution in modern Russia.

Which is fitting, given the importance monumental art held in the former Soviet Union. Lenin's "Monumental Propaganda" plan created state-level demand for a particular style of monuments. A whole Soviet School of sculpture developed, emphasizing social significance, heroism, artistic brevity and grand scale. Notable sculptors designed countless urban monuments, which Lenin used to propagate communist ideas. The Soviet Union was *known* for monumental art, so pulling those memorials down was an act of perfect symbolism.

Back in the USA, we currently have our own issues with fallen heroes. The nation, embroiled in a complicated conversation about our racist history, cannot decide what to do with Confederate statues. Some say we should remove these monuments to slavery; others say doing so would be an affront to history, not to mention that removing monuments—even those celebrating slave-holders—is a slippery slope that would result in our having to denounce Washington, Jefferson, and countless others of our founding fathers. Those points of view both deserve consideration, and they invite broader questions: Who will we commemorate? For how long? Who gets to decide? *Who writes history?*

In Moscow, sculptor Evgeny Chubarov helped answer those questions when he insisted his "heads-in-a-cage" installation in the Park of the Fallen Heroes must be positioned next to the Stalin statue. Chubarov is right: Art can educate through context.

We construct histories and monuments, and we must therefore take responsibility for considering a wide range of perspectives and sometimes even for re-envisioning history. Most of America's Civil War monuments, for example, were not erected until decades after the war had ended. Why erect monuments to the losing side, anyway—what country *ever* does that, once the war is over? Is our Civil War over? Actually, the time period when the monuments were erected corresponds closely with the era of Jim Crow segregation between the 1890s and 1950s. And during that time the placement of new monuments was changed from cemeteries, where they had usually been situated, to state buildings and city squares, where they could teach values—such as glorification of the Civil War. Today they might best be used, as the Stalin statue was, to deepen the impact of new memorials to the thousands of immigrants, slaves, servants and foot soldiers who gave their lives to build this nation. That's the kind of context we need to provide.

It won't be easy. The slope is, indeed, slippery. Patience has worn thin. Tempers flare. Despite their physical size, monuments are only one small part of the huge problem we need to fix. But questioning our inherited symbols—as Chubarov and many others have done—is one way we can start. Those statues are echoes of voices from the past. We must not let them drown out our own conversations.

The Call of the Nightjar

Guppies, white powder, and enlightenment in the dark

Miles from civilization, I sit on a scratched-up plastic chair and swat at flying insects that buzz around my face. Already the night sky burns bright with stars, the Milky Way cutting a sparkling swath through the darkness. Cicadas and crickets buzz nearby, tree frogs call in counterpoint. I can't begin to separate the sounds of all the insects, toads, geckos, and night-calling birds, let alone identify them.

Nigel, on the other hand, is in his element. He's a Trinidadian biologist who was educated in the US. After earning his PhD in integrative biology at UC Berkeley, Nigel conducted research at UC Davis, the Oregon National Primate Research Center, and the US Fish and Wildlife Service. But his true love is the work he's doing where he grew up, on the Caribbean island of Trinidad.

I have volunteered here for a couple of weeks on an Earthwatch research program Nigel is co-directing, both because I love the rainforest and because I hope to learn about the animals living in this habitat, especially the ocelots. What I don't know is that Nigel will also teach me about economics, agriculture, and even philosophy.

"Listen!" he says, knowing I don't understand the strange, musical language all around us. "That's the call of the nightjar." It's right over there. Nigel points into the forest.

The call—deep, clear and liquid—is one of the most distinctive sounds of the night, a kind of *chuck-weep-wit-WEE-oh, chuck-weep-wit-WEE-oh*. It's loud, too; the nightjar is nearby.

"I've been wanting to see one!" I turn my head and peer into the darkness. The nightjar is an odd, nocturnal bird. A plain-looking, brown-and-white ground dweller, it has a well-developed sense of smell—unusual in the avian world. And it's named for its "jarring" call, which I'd been listening to for hours every night since I'd arrived. In fact, it had been keeping me awake. But I couldn't find the bird during the day.

"Oh, you pass right by him every morning," Nigel says. "They're very well camouflaged, but easy to catch. You can often walk right up to one and pick it up—

if you can find him. Maybe I can show you one tomorrow."

This evening, after a long, hot day spent cataloging plants in the rainforest, Nigel and I are relaxing back at camp. During the day he's my boss, assigning sectors of the forest in which we'll document the vegetation, pointing out ocelot scat and subtle trails, and showing us the best places to situate camera traps so we can track the movements of wildlife.

But right now we're having a more personal conversation—Nigel is telling me about his experiences working with the pharmaceutical industry, the surprising importance of this particular part of the rainforest, and how challenging it is to make a living as a research scientist.

"So, do you support yourself doing research projects?" I ask.

Nigel laughs.

He pauses for a long time.

Finally he looks down and says, "I run."

"You run?"

"For a living," he says. "To support myself and my wife and child, who live back in the States." Nigel, who has decided that pharmaceutical-backed research is not a good fit for him, supports his family by extreme running—an endurance sport tougher than ultra-marathoning, with an emphasis on almost unimaginable distances, temperatures, and elevations —and treacherous terrain. He used to win enough prize money from extreme running to support his research. "But now, in my forties, I'm competing with people young enough to be my children." Nigel laughs again, ruefully. "It isn't sustainable."

Sustainability, I will soon learn, is an obsession for Nigel.

Trinidad is home to more than 400 species of birds, as well as a wide variety of exotic tropical animals: ocelots and monkeys, leatherback turtles and boa constrictors, anteaters, agouti and more. The island is a kaleidoscope of biodiversity, which is reason enough to love it, but there's something very special about the streams of Trinidad's northern mountain ranges, especially if you're a biologist ....

It's the guppies. "They're an incredible resource!" Nigel says.

Surely I misunderstood him. These quickly-reproducing aquarium fish sold for ten cents each at the pet store when I was a kid; they can't possibly be of any significant value. But it turns out that Nigel knows a lot more about guppies—and value—than I do.

He explains that the streams here, similar yet geographically isolated from each other, have created a unique natural laboratory. The guppies living in the streams have been studied and documented for many generations, giving scientists an unparalleled ability to learn about the ways evolution and ecology are intertwined.

"These streams have been epicenters for break-throughs in evolutionary theory," Nigel says. "For example, some guppies evolve to be especially swift swimmers, like sprinters. But not all of them do, even though it makes sense evolutionarily for them to be fast, to escape predators."

"OK; why is that?" I ask, swatting at a persistent mosquito and feeling a bit like a predator myself. It raises interesting questions: If speedy guppies are best at escaping predators, why didn't all guppies evolve to be fast? "What other factors come into play?"

"That's what we're learning. The unique combination of isolation, species diversity, and system-replication has allowed scientists to learn a lot about cognition, cooperation and lifespan."

"That sounds like valuable information ..."

"Yes, and that's what it's all about—*value assignment!*" Nigel interrupts me, nearly jumping out of his chair. I've stumbled onto his favorite topic. "Data from Trinidad's streams has powerful implications for models of evolution and conservation, as well as population management. So the northern range of Trinidad has an extraordinarily high global scientific value."

Nigel is educating me, eagerly, hungrily, his words rushing and tumbling like the waterfalls in those mountain streams. He is fascinated with the way people—especially people in power—assign value to various things, from scientific data to food and medicine. This obsession is bigger than his current research, bigger than the rainforest. It's about the very core of sustainable life on Earth.

"Value assignment tends to have cultural bias," he continues, leaning forward in his chair. "It's even a problem for local scientists. The best and brightest go to industrialized countries for their education, and don't learn *tropical* environmental management. If they return to Trinidad, it's often with values reflecting the cultural biases of their white, First-World instructors—including monoculture agriculture."

"What? How is monoculture agriculture a bias?" I grew up in southern Iowa, with its green hills and rolling fields of corn and soybeans. The family farms there are not a bias; they're a tradition.

"We think of farmers as people who till the land," he continues, "because farming is mostly mechanized, computerized. But think about it: We can get only a tenth of the edible produce from monoculture, compared with a mixed-use agri-forest system. Which, by the way, describes the backyards of a lot of people living in the tropics.

"But what about a coffee or banana or cacao plantation," I frown. "Aren't they efficient enough to provide a lot of income?"

"There's a huge demand for caffeine, in the form of coffee, and organizations like the Rainforest Alliance have tried to make coffee agriculture much more sustainable by verifying operations and informing consumers. But these are short-term benefits; there are more nuanced ways of looking at it.

"Another perspective," Nigel continues, "is that when you're marketing coffee—little caffeine packets —it's legalized drug trafficking. People can't subsist on coffee. Even the people who grow it can't subsist on it. They have to export it. They're locked into a specific economic package, which is dependent on the whims and the addictions of people who are wealthy enough to buy it. Is this really a sustainable practice? We have to think longer-term."

"Nigel," I interrupt, "You're giving me a real education—a reeducation."

"No," he insists. "I'm just reminding you of something you already know. People in the First World know this. They realize it when they're pushing paper at their desks, or sitting in traffic..." Nigel trails off, perhaps thinking about the traffic in Berkeley. Then he starts up again.

"It's important to pay attention to what you already know. In marketing we literally create jobs for people to move a perception around. And those are the jobs that make the most money right now—those are the most valuable jobs. Those are the jobs people seek."

Nigel is right; this is information I already have. But now I'm thinking about it in a new way. I shift in my seat. We don't know each other very well. This doesn't seem like the right time to mention that I supported myself and my son for many years on the back of one of those valuable marketing jobs—but I am definitely thinking about it.

Perhaps Nigel senses my discomfort. He leans forward in his chair and changes the subject. "A lot of the perceived value of the rainforest has to do with the potential revenue for big discoveries. You know that the white powders all came from the rainforest."

"The white powders?"

"Yes: sugar, arrowroot, cocaine. Did you know it was legal to buy heroin from Sears Roebuck at the beginning of the twentieth century, and that LSD research was once leading-edge science? There are stigmas attached to them now, but over time we change our attitudes about various chemicals, about certain drugs. Sugar, caffeine, and theobromine—that's chocolate—they're all legally marketed now."

"But what is sustainable in the long term?" Nigel

continues. "Cacao is native to South America and now grows in Africa and around the world. Is it sustainable to expand cacao in Western Africa at the exclusion of native species? People can *look* at a cacao forest and see that it's less diverse than a rainforest."

Nigel stands and begins pacing, his long arms wheeling in the night air. "With a monoculture we're assigning value based on one product or one crop, and the decisions we make are based on the global marketplace, not a local marketplace. The result is increased output—but in non-sustainable way: we move water around, we use pesticides, we poison the earth. So we're decreasing production and increasing management of temporary market value to make a few people very wealthy. Meanwhile, local people can't afford to feed themselves; it's cheaper for them to buy grapes at the supermarket than to grow their own. This is how it works in the global marketplace, where the drive is to *market* something. So you will forfeit subsistence to commute to a place where you can move this valueless information, which sequesters wealth."

The night is still hot and I squirm again, my damp legs sticking to the plastic chair. Sequestering wealth, drug trafficking, benefiting from valueless information—suddenly I feel like one of the bad guys. I'm beginning to understand the nuances Nigel referred to.

"Think of a diamond miner," he suggests. "From the miner's perspective, the diamonds he extracts from the earth are barely valuable enough to provide a subsistence living. But the value of a diamond increases dramatically based on the cultural assignment we give it in the First World. It's just a stone, and not even all that rare, but diamonds are worth a huge amount of money."

"What does the diamond miner have to do with the guppies?" I ask, taken aback by this new tack. Talking with Nigel is like wrangling those guppies; ideas dart every which-way, twisting around on themselves and diving off again in a new direction.

"Studying the ecology of wild guppies has led to insights about health care, behavioral models, and the design of cooperative networks," he continues. "These applications are assigned high values in the global marketplace."

"So there's a high value in terms of both science and commerce! That's a good thing; value assignment is working the way it should."

"Yes, but the rainforest is disappearing because of the value assessment of businesses and the voting public in Trinidad. They think the jungle is only good for recreation, tourism, and cheap resource extraction."

I think I understand what Nigel is talking about. This is one of the things Earthwatch notes as a bright surprise about their research: Having citizen scientists come from around the world to study a place often makes the local people value things they had previously taken for granted.

"There are so many treasures hidden here," I begin, as the nightjar calls again. *Chuck-weep-wit-WEE-oh, chuck-weep-wit-WEE-oh.* "There's a whole medicine cabinet in the jungle. Maybe there's even a cure for cancer. If we would only appreciate what we have and preserve it..."

Nigel interrupts, choosing his words carefully: "The potential to discover cancer-curing drugs is not the only reason—or even the best reason—to preserve the rainforest," he explains haltingly, pausing to let his point sink in. He sits down again and looks out into the night—not at me. "That's a white, First-World reason."

"What do you mean, *It's a white, First-World reason?*" It seems like Nigel is accusing me of something, but I'm not sure what. I feel vaguely guilty. The conversation is awkward for both of us.

"The rainforest can have much more value than just being a grab bag for potential cures for cancer," Nigel explains. "Cancer is a minor problem for the wealthiest of the wealthy."

I have no idea what he's talking about. My mother and both my grandmothers died of cancer. It was a pretty big deal to them, and we're certainly not the wealthiest of the wealthy.

"In most of the world, people don't even live long enough to get cancer," Nigel continues. "What they need is food. The rainforest is important because it's a tropical breadbasket." His voice rises in excitement, and the jungle goes silent.

So we're all running around looking for miracle cures, I think, *and ignoring what's right in front of our faces—all the food the rainforest provides. It's the biodiversity that makes living here sustainable. And once we've lost it to monoculture* ... I'm beginning to get the picture. "But how would we assign value to biodiversity?"

"Exactly!" Nigel exclaims. "How *do* we decide what is valuable? What is the value of what is unknown, of what isn't yet discovered? And how do you market it? Here's an example: Before a few years ago there was a relatively unknown fruit called açaí. It got marketed, it was going to cure cancer and a whole lot more."

I remember there was a big marketing push. Curing cancer was just the beginning; açaí was an anti-aging miracle. It was supposed to improve our heart health and immune systems, plus make us thinner, sexier, and smarter.

"The hype went up; the hype went down. Antioxidants do what antioxidants do. By the way, most of these super-foods that we value are actually poisons in a certain dose. That's why they're antimicrobial, because the plant is trying to kill whatever is attempting to eat it. Everything is a double-edged sword. Kale and blueberries, for example, developed to be mild toxins, or to inhibit digestion until a seed passes through."

"So the açaí..." I begin, endeavoring to pull Nigel back on track.

"Açaí suddenly had a huge value. We assign value only in terms of money, but we can expand how we think about it."

What Nigel's saying makes sense. Food is valuable, but so is scientific research. We may not realize its value for generations, though, and we can't put a number on it.

"What is the value of figuring out why some guppies become sprinters?" Nigel asks. "Or of knowing what determines their life span—or yours? Or finding a cure for cancer? There's so much we haven't discovered!"

I look at him quizzically. *Does Nigel realize what he just said?* Then we both burst into laughter.

"OK; I admit it," he chuckles. "I had to throw in *cure for cancer.*"

We gaze up at the night sky. I don't know what Nigel is thinking, but I'm contemplating my new understanding of the value of the rainforest. Nigel has led me into a maze as big as the forest itself: sustainability, the ecology of wild guppies, evolutionary theory, marketing and value assignment, cultural bias, diamond mining, agricultural science, biodiversity, a cure for cancer, blueberries, and açaí.

Here in the rainforest, under the night sky, it all comes together in an *ah-ha* moment that feels as expansive as the Milky Way. This beautiful, diverse ecosystem is more than its coffee and cacao, more than its tourist-attracting monkeys and ocelots—more, even than its capacity to feed and heal people. It exists for itself, not as a benefit to humans. And it's home to the nightjar.

Chuck-weep-wit-WEE-oh!

A Voyeur in Libya

A photographic invasion leads to indelible regret

A little girl squints up with an impossibly sweet half-smile, the hot pink of her shirt reflecting up onto her rosy cheeks. She stands arm-in-arm with her little brother who looks about three and has a headful of curly black hair and big brown eyes. His white T-shirt is decorated with a lively illustration of flowers and cherries formed into a heart, and his cherubic cheeks beg to be pinched. The two children's heads lean in, touching. They clasp one another's henna-painted hands. These little ones look happy and completely unselfconscious, as though they pose like this for strangers on a regular basis. Maybe they do.

We are in the grand medina in Tripoli, a confusing warren of twisting lanes and alleyways lined with shops and apartments. I was lucky enough to get into Libya with an educational travel group during one of the slivers of time when it was open to Americans, and its capital city is a captivating mix of archaeology, coffee shops, and modern architecture. Today I have ventured into the medina alone to explore, take some photos, and buy a souvenir or two.

Above, the sky is blistering blue. Inside the medina, the colors are even more dazzling. Elaborate gold necklaces sparkle seductively; silver and copper bowls glint in the sunshine. Fantastically bejeweled dresses, both Libyan and Western-style, hang on rows of Caucasian mannequins. Mounds of every imaginable hue of orange and yellow spices create bright mandalas. The scents of green herbs and cedarwood, strong coffee, tobacco smoke and jasmine blossoms coalesce into an irresistible perfume, enticing me deeper and deeper into the tight tangle of narrow, stall-lined passages until I am happily lost in the medina's labyrinth. A tailor sits off to the side of one lane, his treadle sewing machine humming as he constructs a sturdy shopping bag from blue-and-white plaid fabric. Around the corner, scissors click as a barber wearing a bright green T-shirt plies his trade in the middle of the alleyway. Nearby, five boys huddle around a broken stick-hockey table, goofing off, trying to make it work. Arabic music wails from a boom box sitting on the ground next to them. The road is muddy from an early-morning rain.

All this stimulation makes me greedy—eager to touch every piece of silky fabric, to photograph every bulging sack of turmeric, every intricately painted plate, every conjunction of azure sky and stately palm and ancient arch. Here is a necklace my mother would love. *Click*. There is a taxidermied hare smoking a hookah. Huh? *Click!* Next to it is a stack of sparkling bracelets. I am *click-click-click*-ing away when the sound of a small scuffle interrupts my concentration. Then a soft giggle.

The little boy and girl have adopted me! Still holding hands, they tag along as I move through the medina with my camera, memorializing a perfectly symmetrical stack of glazed pastries here, a row of bright lamé fabrics there. Wait! A pickup truck loaded with camels creeps by. *Click-click*. A table of colorful glass perfume bottles glows in the afternoon light. *Click-click-click*. It's nearly time to rendezvous with the group, and our mini-bus will not wait. I'm not with a guide, don't speak Arabic, and could be getting myself into real trouble ... *but I can't ... must not ... miss a shot.*

The children, who are waving at me now, have tagged along for several blocks. What if they get lost? They're certainly not afraid of strangers. And they're adorable. I'd like to get a picture of them—their easy friendliness, their shy-but-eager approach. Is it OK to photograph kids who are on their own? I lift my camera slightly, and they smile. They want me to take the shot. Am I supposed to tip them—do they make a regular income this way? I raise my camera to my eye. Do their parents worry about the youngsters, alone in the medina? Is there time before the bus leaves? If I miss it, how will I get back to the hotel? I click a grab-shot and run for the bus, feeling off-balance, a little predatory, afraid I'm doing something wrong.

I am a voyeur, looking but not interacting.

The same feeling had crept in that very morning as I walked through the medina, photographing into stores and restaurants. It would have seemed awkward to hang around, trying to make friends for a day. I don't speak their language and besides, the shopkeepers were at work. It can be complicated, figuring out how to photograph strangers in a country where I don't know the customs and can barely get myself from point A to point B, which is how it is here in Libya. Best to just get my shots as unobtrusively as possible and move along.

Sometimes my subject has no interest in interacting, but also doesn't motion me away. Earlier on this Libya trip I took photos of three separate men with wrinkled brown faces staring straight at me, impassively, neither accepting nor rejecting my photographic advances. Are photographs like that consensual? They all came out looking a little scary.

The younger men were simple to shoot. Most wore Western clothing, but some were in robes. They stopped and smiled, making eye contact easily as they went about their daily business: selling dresses or necklaces, waiting tables, talking on their cell phones, taking a cigarette break. It didn't matter that we communicated only with gestures—a smile, raised eyebrows, my camera held aloft in a silent question.

At the ancient ruins at Cyrene on Libya's Mediterranean shore I met two Libyan women. I'd been focusing on an 1,800-year-old mosaic with gorgeous floral patterns when they walked by in black robes, their heads covered with *hijabs*, their faces fully exposed. I held up my camera and pantomimed "May I take your photo?"

The two women stopped and smiled. It was clearly OK. One waited patiently while the other pulled the loose ends of her black scarf up to completely cover her face. Not even her eyes showed from behind her veil. She posed that way until I'd snapped a few times. I lowered the camera. She lowered the fabric and smiled again in easy camaraderie.

Later that day I handed my camera to a stranger

and asked him to take a photo of me with three local men I'd been "communicating" with as we explored the ruins. They were in their forties, wore Western clothing, and spoke a few words of English.

"Hello."

"Where you from?"

"Beautiful day."

The four of us lined up in front of an ancient sandstone column and I threw my arm around the man on my right and smiled for the camera. That evening I reviewed the shots and was horrified to see that the man I had my arm around looked positively ill; I'd apparently made a terrible social error by touching him. He'd been too polite to object at the time, but his face and body language clearly communicated the extent of my mistake.

Once, in Paris, I'd made a similar faux pas. I saw a beautiful, fresh-faced young couple walking together in the late afternoon. The woman carried a glossy pink shopping bag—big and obviously heavy, as though she'd been on a spree. The light was perfect: warm and golden. The name of the store, emblazoned in bold black letters on the side of the bag, was *A-c-n-e. Acne!* I didn't know, at the time, that Acne Studios was a stylish Swedish company whose name is an acronym for Associated Computer Nerd Enterprises. It wouldn't have mattered if I did; the ironic juxtaposition was too good to pass up. I chased after the couple, angling to get a good view of the *Acne* on the side of the bag. The man realized what was going on and quickly positioned himself between me and his companion, protecting her. Maybe she was someone famous, and expertly fending off paparazzi came along with the job, whatever job he had. Or perhaps they were having an affair and my photographing them was intrusive for that reason. *Or maybe the man simply didn't want to have his picture taken.* Who knows? He glared at me. I didn't care. I was hungry for the shot.

Actually, he never asked me to stop shooting. That doesn't matter, though. If they felt I was being intrusive, then I was being intrusive, and I should have stopped ... but I didn't. I got the shot—and felt sleazy doing it. I knew I had crossed a line.

Many of the photos I've taken around the world now hang on my walls at home. The two children from the medina smile down from a framed print, eighteen by twenty-four inches of angelic innocence. The tailor with his blue-and-white shopping bag is there, along with the stick-hockey boys, an old man drinking coffee, and the smiling shopkeeper with his row of blond mannequins. But I never printed the Acne couple, or myself with the three men from Cyrene. Those photos remain hidden in my camera, evoking a shudder every time I accidentally come across them—which is why I keep them. As a penance. A reminder. A secret talisman against the times when I'm tempted to cross the line, to steal something instead of asking for and accepting a remembrance, an invitation generously given into another's world—one of travel's greatest gifts.

Transformation

Cuba Through the Looking Glass

A single artist transforms an entire village

A long blue pool stretches across the center of the compound. It is surrounded by tall palm trees and slippery, red-lipped fish. Looking down from his home above the water, a laughing monkey sits atop the pregnant giraffe's back. Roosters spread their wings in the sun. Nearby, a gigantic strawberry-and-pistachio sundae with a cherry on top melts in the bright December light. There is no sound.

I move silently, glad I wore my sneakers. It's still early, and I don't want to disturb the residents or draw attention to myself as I climb to the third story of the compound for a better look.

Cowboys are everywhere. One wears heavy black mascara and blood-red lipstick. There is a fish where his heart should be. Another cowboy rides off on a dragon, his long blue cape blowing in the breeze. The mermaid in his arms does not look happy to be there; I think perhaps he is kidnapping her. A third cowboy stands, motionless, holding his bright red crutches. I skirt them all, one after another, making my way quickly to the top of the building where a huge red woman awaits, a golden sunflower sprouting from her head. Her tiny breasts poke out impertinently. The left one is bigger than the right. I lie down at the woman's feet and marvel at the deep blue beyond, a sky so clear and bright it reaches down, wraps itself around the woman, and then envelopes me, too, in its indigo intensity.

This is Fusterlandia, a zany wonderland created by José Rodriguez Fuster over the course of more than forty years ... and he's still building it. Fuster's work has been compared with Gaudí's, Picasso's and Dubuffet's, and it's easy to see their influences in his fanciful mosaics, double-faced women and colorful naïve renderings. The renowned Cuban artist began by covering his own studio—a small wooden house in the seaside town of Jaimanitas—with colorful paintings and mosaics. When Fuster ran out of walls, he filled the yard with psychedelic sculptures: mermaids, palm trees, roosters and gigantic disembodied hands. Then he moved on, with permission, to cover more than eighty of his neighbors' houses with wildly ornate sculpture, painting and mosaic art. He was unstoppable, eventually decorating roofs, walls, gates, doorways, bus stops, benches and fountains.

Of course it wasn't just fun and games. When José Fuster first began expanding Fusterlandia in the town of Jaimanitas, the locals weren't all immediately appreciative. But that soon changed: It seems Fuster's effervescent spirit—his joy in creation—was irresistible. His art transformed an economically depressed village, well off the beaten track, into a fantasyland that attracts busloads of curious travelers. It's free to enter Fusterlandia, and it's easy to spend a little money on a souvenir tile or a painting in one of the many gift shops nearby. The whole town has benefitted—and bootstrapped itself to greater prosperity—as a result of Fuster's vision.

Near the red woman with a sunflower sprouting from her head I find the vantage point I am searching for. It's the epicenter of Fuster's kaleidoscopic dreamscape, and gives me a clear view of his Madonna. Rays of golden light emanate from her head as she clutches the child and a cross. To the Madonna's left, a green octopus waves its tentacles wildly. The three men carrying her in a rowboat do not seem concerned. Overhead, gigantic headless snakes curl, like sinuous rollercoasters, in dizzying loop-de-loops. A golden-eyed crocodile balances a bottle of beer on its back.

I spot a bench that is covered with white ceramic

tiles and decorated with red hearts and blue flowers. Across the back is painted, in a childlike scrawl, *La alegria de vivir.* The joy of living. This is the first message of Fusterlandia.

Fuster credits the time he spent teaching literacy skills in the Sierra Maestra, a mountainous region of southeastern Cuba, for inspiring his art. The peasants, palm trees and crocodiles of that area still show up now—decades later—in his work. After that teaching experience in his late teens, Fuster trained for two years at the National School for Art Instructors in Havana. He's been working as a professional artist ever since. I am surprised to learn that "artist" is a state-approved profession, and it turns out that Cuba treats its artists well. Fidel Castro recognized early on that selling art—which is exempted from the trade embargo—was one of the few legal ways to get US money into the country.

Cuban artists enjoy the same free education as students in other fields, and the subject is taken seriously. Printmaking, for example, has been an independent specialty in the education system since 1959. And in 1962, a printmaking collective was founded in Old Havana.

That collective, the Taller Experimental de Gráfica, is still standing, and it is one of my favorite places to visit. Even though it's run by the state, the Taller isn't a big warehouse full of food-rationing booklets or political propaganda. It's an enormous bunker-like cement building with high windows and a rough interior, and it's filled with art—really *good* art.

Near the entrance, just to the left, are the dancing coffeepots. In portrait after portrait they pose, often in pairs, bowing, primping and swishing; puffing themselves up to look more important; arguing, kibitzing or demurring. They get along fine without legs, and their heads often become daffodils.

I walk up the aisle, passing long tables loaded with paint samples—red, yellow, blue, green, orange—buckets, rollers, stacks of prints. I know where I'm headed: to a display of brightly colored, hand-painted-and-burnished prints. They're clipped up to horizontal strings in an improvised booth, to surround the viewer. The images are wild and beautiful, frightening in their intensity—a green cat, red and yellow stripes, fish with stars for eyes, darling hooves, blue reptilian skin—all layered into an exploding mythology unlike anything I have ever seen. Loaded with symbolism and gold foil, these pieces magnetize me from across the room and make my heart beat faster.

On one visit I meet a printmaker named Alejandro. He has worked at the Taller for twenty-six years and has a headful of wild hair, a charming gap between his front teeth, and speaks English well. Alejandro shows me several serigraphs in the series he is working on—colorful depictions of men in big, round, deep-sea diving helmets.

In one print, four divers labor beneath the water, harvesting seaweed with machetes. They wear orange diving suits and yellow helmets. Although they inhabit the same seabed, each diver is distinct, separated from the others, unable to communicate except perhaps with a few arm signals. Bubbles drift upwards, bright white circles against the dark kelp forest. Above the men—on the surface of the sea—a man relaxes in a rowboat, unaware of the alternate reality below. The style is completely different from that in Fusterlandia, but there's a haunting similarity in their imageries: innocent subjects in bright Caribbean colors distracting—at first—from a subtler message that things are more complicated than they first appear.

In another of Alejandro's serigraphs, a farmer ploughs his field in the slanting afternoon sun. It looks quietly idyllic until I realize the beast of burden is not an ox, but a rhinoceros. In a third print, a diver is wrapped in the red-white-and-blue Cuban flag, with a big red shield and the white Cuban star emblazoned over his heart. With up to eleven colors each, the prints are bright, lively and technically excellent.

Alejandro holds up the print of the four deep-sea divers to give me a better look.

"What's going on in this one?" I ask.

"These images show the difficulty of what we do every day," Alejandro says. "It's like we are living underwater, with limited oxygen, and every movement requires extra energy."

"That's what it feels like, living in Cuba?"

"That's what it feels like every day."

Once Alejandro has told me what the images mean to him, I realize those feelings have crept into me, too, as I view the divers: the claustrophobia of living underwater, the heaviness, the isolation. The fear just a breath away. I try to imagine what it would be like to have those feelings every day.

Since we're getting personal, I decide it might be OK to ask Alejandro a little more about how the financial system works in Cuba. "Do you earn a salary for your work here?" I venture.

"Yes, of course!" he replies, looking a little bewildered.

I feel both foolish and incredulous—it's hard to believe the government would pay printmakers to create art—not government publications, but *art. Any art. Whatever they want.* No one seems to be looking over Alejandro's shoulder, telling him not to show what it looks like to live underwater, not to comment on the extra energy required for everyday activities. It's true that there was censorship in the early '70s, but since then things have opened up. Since the '90s, Cuban art has included more explicitly political content and even critiques of the Revolution.

"And do you also get paid when the prints are sold?" I ask, still finding it hard to comprehend the extent of this government-funded enterprise.

"Yes, we get to keep seventy percent of the sale price; the government gets the other thirty percent to pay for the space—it's expensive to keep the lights on and do regular maintenance."

The Taller Experimental de Gráfica is not the only art hot-spot in Havana. The Museum of Cuban Art displays world-class painting; the Fabrica de Arte Cubano combines art, fashion and music; and many of the streets in Old Havana—especially Empedrado—are home to quirky little galleries and individual artists' studios: A super-realist paints faux broken panes of glass over his seascapes. A portrait artist evokes intense anguish with black-and-white faces. A photographer specializes in the upside- down worlds reflected in water.

Even the graffiti and street art in Cuba are full of symbolism and mystery. Yulier Rodriguez, who signs his work Julier P, has populated the streets of Old Havana with space-alien-like creatures: bald, big-headed beings whose body parts aren't assembled properly. Many include visual references to hunger: creatures with many breasts, or mouthless ones. Some critics speculate that the mouthlessness implies a lack of voice and refers to artistic censorship. That's certainly possible; the police keep track of Rodriguez's work, and subjected him to an interview about it. They didn't arrest him, though. The Cuban constitution guarantees his right to create art—as long as it doesn't oppose the Revolution.

Another artist, who works semi-anonymously, paints a balaclava-clad character accompanied by the phrase "2 + 2 = 5." I ask Yoli, our local guide, what that means—maybe *Something isn't adding up?* She asks friends, but no one seems to know.

Later I read an article that said the signature phrase was a direct reference to a line in Orwell's *1984*: "In the end the Party would announce that two and two made five, and you would have to believe it.... Not merely the validity of experience, but the very existence of external reality, was tacitly denied by their philosophy." Of course, that could refer as easily to the our recent administration's claims about "fake news" and "alternative facts" as to Cuban censorship.

But the artist himself is circumspect, perhaps because that is still the safest stance. In one interview he is quoted as saying the phrase is simply a childhood nickname; in another he says it represents freedom: "People say that two plus two equals four, but I don't see it like that. I believe that it can equal whatever you want it to be. You can be whatever you want to be... And I want people to know that, so I put it everywhere with my art. I paint here, I paint there, I paint everywhere. I want people to know that I am free."

I've been thinking a lot about Cuban art since my conversation with Alejandro. Its generally naïve style, frequently fantastical subject matter and usually inoffensive approach might seem to say, *Don't take me seriously.* But underneath, for those who know how to read them, other messages await. Cuban artists express themselves in code; their work speaks on multiple levels. A second monkey perches on the elephant's head. The woman's body becomes a cross.

2 + 2 = 5.

At the Foot of Uluru

Learning to see in the forest of snotty gobbles

My socks are thick and my boots are sturdy. I am ready to climb Uluru. That's the Aboriginal name for the gigantic red monolith that is Australia's iconic landmark. Also called Ayers Rock in honor of Henry Ayers, the Australian who "discovered" it in 1873, Uluru rises 1,140 feet—more than 100 stories—above the continent's flat central desert, where humans have lived for as many as 60,000 years.

I've long dreamed of climbing this towering sandstone formation, and now here I am in Australia's Red Center, where it's located, hundreds of miles from what most people today consider civilization. My hotel at Yulara, half an hour away from the actual sacred site, has provided 5:30 a.m. shuttle service and a small plastic bottle of water. My dream is about to come true.

Most of the ride, along with a coach full of other passengers, was in the dark, but we arrived in time to disembark a mile or so away and view Uluru at sunrise, its magnificent form morphing from brown to rusty red to brilliant vermillion as the morning dawned. From this distance it looks like a postcard, bright red against a bluing sky, except that the colors seem to be alive—fluid—changing from moment to moment in the waxing light. The deep craters running down the island mountain's side are invisible at first, but begin to appear, ghostlike, as the sun casts shadows on its edges.

We re-board the shuttle. I'm glad to get going again, eager to get to Uluru and begin my climb before the day gets too hot. I want to be inspired. I want to feel the effort in my legs and lungs—to see far across the flat, dry expanse of bunchgrass and shrubs, all the way to voluptuous Kata Tjuta, Uluru's sister formation thirty-six miles away. Bragging rights would be nice, too.

We arrive to discover the base of Uluru littered with a ragtag collection of warning signs, in all different sizes and colors and lettering, apparently erected over time as new hazards presented themselves.

Stay on the marked track at all times, one sign says.

Wear sun protection, a second directs.

They do not discourage me. I've lived in Australia

for more than a year, and have been indoctrinated by the country's "Slip, Slop, Slap" public service ad campaign, so I know to slip on a long-sleeved shirt, slop on the sunscreen, and slap on a hat for sun protection.

The most prominent sign says: *Be sure to bring plenty of water. Drink one litre for every hour you walk.* This calls for some quick calculations. The climb takes two to three hours, round-trip, so three liters of water, minimum ... hmm ... that's nearly a gallon, quite a lot of weight to haul up.

Many people have died or been injured attempting to climb Uluru, yet another marker proclaims. Winds can be high, and there's absolutely no shade to offer adventurers respite from the desert sun. It isn't uncommon for tourists to be injured, stranded, or lost in one of the deep-walled crevices, requiring a rescue helicopter.

At the base of the rock are five small bronze plaques, each dedicated to someone who died attempting an ascent. One reads:

In memory of Brian Joseph Miller
Who died from a fall while
Climbing Ayers Rock on May 18th 1978, Age 25
Sad loss to Jack and Jean Miller
Brothers Keith and Peter

Age twenty-five. Yes, that would surely be a sad loss.

I spot yet another sign that warns: *Don't Risk Your Life! People die here every year.* There have been nearly forty recorded deaths on Uluru since the government started keeping track. Most are from heart attacks.

None of these signs deter me. But one small plaque manages to stop me in my tracks:

We do not climb.

The local Anangu people, who are traditional caretakers of this land, request that visitors refrain from clambering over this sacred place. The inconspicuous plaque explains that their ancestral law forbids such behavior.

Not everyone heeds this sign. In 2010 a footballer boasted that he'd hit a golf ball from the top of the rock in solidarity with a controversial twenty-five-year-old

French woman who, earlier that year, had filmed herself doing a striptease atop Uluru. "I could feel zee good energy of zee place," she said in one of many subsequent interviews. "And I just needed to ... to ... *express* myself." Which she did—in a white-fringed bikini and dusty cowboy boots.

The Health Minister for the Northern Territory responded with an apt analogy: "How would French people feel if an Australian danced semi-naked on the altar of Notre Dame?"

We do not climb.

This is my only chance to conquer Uluru—to stand atop it, feel the wind, see across the desert for miles and miles. Yet the sign makes a good point, and I want to be respectful.

On the other hand, I will be riding back to the hotel this evening with people who *did* make the ascent. They will be

comparing notes about their climb times, the state of their aching feet, and whether or not they carried enough water. They will be discussing the stultifying heat and the magnificent view, exalting in the fact that they have fulfilled a lifelong dream and can finally check this *totally awesome* experience off their bucket lists. Sitting in the bus with them all the way back to the hotel will be torture.

As we approach the base of Uluru I can see that some people have already begun their climbs. This massive inselberg is extremely steep in places. Heavy chains have been installed as handholds, pounded into the body of the sandstone, assisting as a parade of people scramble up the access route. Over the years, their boots have created a long gray scar marking the ascent.

The climbers are perfectly spaced, like a line of ants at a picnic—a determined band of ants who have found a food source and are leading their compatriots to it. What kind of nourishment do they expect atop Uluru? They move in a slow-motion frenzy, and suddenly I realize I want no part of it.

That's when I spot the white "Uluru Experience" van. It's parked at the side of the road, positioned to pick off stragglers like myself, people who are having second thoughts about climbing.

A skinny-legged young man with a soft brown afro climbs out of the van. He looks like a ranger in his hiking boots and khaki shirt and shorts, and is about the same age as Brian Joseph Miller was when he lost his life to Uluru in 1978.

"G'day. I'm David," he says. "I can take you on a walk here at base of Uluru, if you like. We'll see native plants and animals, and you'll learn how the Anangu people have been able to survive in this harsh environment." I sign up for the tour, along with three other visitors.

David begins right there, at the van, directing our gazes across the desert. "What do you see?" he asks. "Any food? Nothing but porcupine grass and shrubs? Look again. See the wildflowers?"

We all stare dumbly for a minute.

"There's one!" I say finally, pointing to the only spot of color I can find: a fleck of magenta a hundred feet away.

David shoos away a persistent fly. "That's pigface. It can be eaten raw or boiled, the juice can be applied to sand fly bites, and the leaves can be crushed into a poultice for healing burns. And this is a honey locust." He directs our attention to the blossoms that are beginning to appear, like magic, as we look at the landscape more closely. We see a yellow crepe-papery flower that looks like a hibiscus, and something called bloodwood—David says it indicates the presence of shallow groundwater.

At this point David pulls an armful of thin, graceful containers from the back of the van, passing them around for us to hold. They are lightweight but hard, about fifteen inches long, and polished smooth by years of use. These *coolamons* were carved from tree trunks. They were traditionally used by Aboriginal women to carry water or grass seeds—or even to cradle babies. He lifts a seedpod carefully from one of the bowls. It's beautiful: brown and slender and covered with tiny spikes that must be the seeds. David tells us this is wattleseed. It's super nutritious; the Aboriginals crush it into flour and cook it into cakes or damper. The husks are very hard—they can last for up to twenty years, usually germinating only after a bushfire. "It's a reliable source of food in times of drought," David tells us.

We try out digging sticks of various sizes. These are tools used to dig up roots and grubs. David demonstrates the use of a throwing stick, explaining that it can be used to extend the reach of a spear, and then a boomerang commonly used for hunting game.

"See that little forest?" he asks, pointing directly at Uluru. At first I see only scrubby brush; then I realize that the immensity of the monolithic formation has made the stunted woodland near its base look smaller than its twenty-foot height. There is actually a *forest* at the base of Uluru.

"Those are weeping pittosporums, also known by such colorful names as *gumbi gumbi* and *snotty gobbles*," David explains, wiping his brow. The sun is up, and the day is already getting hot. "That one's a witchetty bush; you've heard of witchetty grubs?"

I've heard of them, all right; every outback tourist has. Witchetty grubs are fat, white worms that burrow into the desert sand like some creature from *Dune*. They supposedly taste like peanut butter, but I am not brave enough to try one. "The grubs are dug up from near the roots of the witchetty bush and eaten raw or cooked. They're very nutritious," David explains. He looks as though he might dig up some witchetty grubs on the spot and pass them around for a taste test. I begin to worry, but fortunately he moves on. "See this spinifex?"

One of the first things I learned in Australia was to beware of the harsh, prickly bunchgrass. It has lacerated my ankles many times, and I hate it.

But David has a different perspective. "The roots are connected in an extensive network that helps stabilize the desert sands. And at certain times of the year the plant produces a sticky sap that's heated up and used as glue. It becomes very hard after it cools. Pretty amazing, right?" He disappears into the back of the white van, then reappears clutching something that's alive. A plump lizard with pretty bands of dusky orange and green across its back wriggles in David's grasp. "This is a goanna, one of several species of monitor lizards found in Australia. The oily white meat tastes like chicken, and they're a good food source because they grow to be five feet long."

This one must be a baby; it's barely eighteen inches, including the tail. Thankfully, we are not offered a sample. David sets the goanna on the ground. The lizard is the exact same colors as the reddish dirt and dusty scrub grasses. It skitters across the sandy earth and vanishes.

David stashes his visual aids—the digging sticks and throwing sticks, the *coolamons* and wattleseed and boomerang—in the van, and we begin a leisurely walk along a wide path that curves around the base of Uluru. Up close, pockmarks, fissures, and caves in the craggy walls create a surprising contrast to Uluru's monolithic appearance from afar.

David drones on like a didgeridoo, telling us that Uluru is sacred to the Aboriginal people, that it evokes the Dreamtime before humans existed, a time when ancestral beings called *Mala* roamed the land having adventures, meeting friends, and performing ceremonies. The gorges, waterholes, and rock formations are physical evidence of those ancient events, as the Mala brought all being into creation.

"This is Kulpi Minymaku, the Kitchen Cave. Women and girls camp here. They go out into the bush to collect *mai*—foods like vegetables, grubs, and honey—while the men hunt for *kuka,* or meat. They have done this for thousands of years. Here's Mala Puta cave, the pouch of the female hare-wallaby—it's very important spiritually. It's taboo to enter or photograph it. Over there is an acacia woodland. See these few small trees? They're bush plums. They aren't a true plum, but they have a stone fruit—mostly stone, a little fruit—that is very nutritious, very high in vitamin C." We continue walking. The heat is oppressive. Dust rises. I sneeze. Flies buzz.

Just when I think I may die from sunstroke, we come across a small pool of water. I feel a breeze.

"Sit quietly and breathe deeply," David says, perching on a small boulder. "Enjoy this moment. This is the real Uluru."

I sit on my own personal boulder and sip some water, then splash a few drops on my face and neck. It evaporates instantly. A beetle skitters through the sand as I slip into the world around me, a land of ancient rivulets and fat lizards, sinew and spirits, rock and song—all essential for survival. A couple of birds sing in the trees and the buzz of cicadas reverberates against Uluru's massive shoulder. Has all this rich mystery opened a liminal world? Have I shifted into the Dreamtime? Dreamtime, when the earth was young, before people were people, when our sisters were snakes and our souls were expansive. A time when no one knew something and everyone knew it all.

I realize David is still talking. "The water is *kapi; kapi* is life. When it rains, thundering waterfalls pour down the cliff. See this black stain?" He traces a finger along the edge of a long, dark blotch that stretches up the face of the rock. "That's algae, growing along the path where water falls. Look into the water; you see *kurtji kurtji*. You call them tadpoles. They must turn into frogs before the *kapi* dries up. What eats the frogs? What eats the bush plums? We're all here for a reason. Each thing has its place."

Yes, I think. *Each thing has its place. Even us.*

As we head back to the van, I realize I'm glad I didn't climb Uluru. A whole forest grows here at Uluru's base—a bit sparse, but a forest nonetheless. Before, I hadn't even noticed it. But with David I'm exploring in a deeper and more respectful way, thinking about every step I take. A goanna could be anywhere, with its perfect camouflage. I see spinifex in a new light: Those prickly blades of grass aren't just pesky ankle irritants. They are protecting the plant, and the plant's extensive roots are integrally important to the fragile desert ecosystem. I am here at the foot of the mountain and for the moment, I'm also part of it—not climbing, not dancing on it. I may not have classic photos from the summit, but I have connected with Uluru, and that connection feels good.

Uluru was permanently closed to climbers in October, 2019. Sammy Wilson, Former Chairman of the Uluru-Kata Tjuta Board of Management, said, "The land has law and culture. We welcome tourists here. Closing the climb is not something to feel upset about, but a cause for celebration. Let's come together; let's close it together."

Dreaming the Minotaur

A labyrinth of discontent leads to profound appreciation

Knossos lies in ruin, yet it is stunning. Blocks of glinting white stone have crumbled to the ground, leaving a sprawling, sugar-cube outline where the palace's walls once towered. Bright red reconstructions replace the original stout cypress columns on endless colonnades; faded frescoes evoke the citadel's elegant past. Once the capital of a flourishing Minoan civilization, this ancient site is now a tourist attraction. I had come to Knossos, on the island of Crete, in search of a labyrinth. Actually, I wanted to find *the* labyrinth—Knossos was said to be home to the world's very first.

I secretly hoped that walking the labyrinth would help me with a life-long problem: difficulty making decisions. My father taught me from the time I was very young to think for myself. But, like many men, he became irritated when my opinion differed from his.

"There are only two answers," he would say. "Mine, and the wrong one." He pretended it was a joke, but it wasn't. Then there was Mom, a genius at looking at every issue from multiple angles. Together they were perfect-storm parents for raising me, a daughter who is skilled at considering endless perspectives, easily intuits what others think ... and second-guesses her own opinions so thoroughly she's often unsure whether she even *has* a personal point of view.

Growing up this way got me thinking about the mysteries of how we know, and how we decide. What are the relative weights of analysis and instinct, the merits of reason and emotion? I hoped that figuring out the interplay between confidence and faith—those two opposing cornerstones of conclusion—would transform my wobbly decision-making abilities. That is what drew me to Knossos.

I would make a pilgrimage to the original labyrinth and have a magical experience there—attending only to earth and sky, feeling the subtleties of air and light as they played off one another, silencing my monkey-mind chatter. I would walk the labyrinth until I felt what I needed: confidence to take the next step, even if I didn't know exactly where I was going, and faith that I could enter the unknown and find a way back out. My indecision would be transformed into certainty!

That was my plan.

Knossos, just a short bus ride from Crete's capital city of Heraklion, is a lovely place to wander. The palace once looked out over rolling hills blanketed with olive groves. Their gnarled descendants still cloak the landscape and are home to finches and flycatchers, to warblers and robins and wrens. Beneath the trees' silvery leaves, golden grasses shimmer in the heat, cicadas thrum, and Queen Anne's lace folds its delicate blossoms into thick vegetal cups.

I arrived in the morning, intending to be in and out before the summer heat became too debilitating. The place was immense. Stone walls outlined the remains of private apartments, interior and exterior courtyards, complex baths, granaries, storage rooms and meeting halls—all linked by wide walkways and the palace's four flights of staircases. Waves of light shimmered, mirage-like, as the sun rose higher in the sky, its bright glare reflecting on acres of white stone. Map in hand, I explored the architecture as it repeated and reflected, twisting in upon itself and confusing even the most observant visitor. But where was the actual labyrinth? I wandered for several hours, looking high and low, gamely following winding pathways, hopefully poking my head over and over again into the same rooms, which looked different from their various approaches.

Finally I realized the truth.

There was no labyrinth at Knossos. In all likelihood, there never had been. The labyrinth I'd turned to for salvation was a myth, just like the Minotaur who supposedly lived inside it. My aspirations puddled in the heat.

Maybe it was the too-bright sunlight, alternating with deep shadows in the porticoed throne room. Perhaps it was the larger-than-life-sized frescoed griffons inside, their graceful lion-bodies and bird-heads detailed with mesmerizing spirals. Or the blue monkey with a long nose, stooping by the side of a river to pluck a tall stalk of papyrus. The frescoes' dreamlike imagery pulled at my imagination as I wandered the ruins. Most of the images were of lotus blossoms and long-limbed courtiers, but one was unique. It depicts an oddly red and freakishly acrobatic youth somersaulting over the back of a huge brown bull—bull-jumping, in the parlance of the time. Two older boys stand nearby, their black hair in long ringlets, their powerful thighs only partly covered by loincloths. One of the boys stands with his arms outstretched, ready to catch the vaulting athlete; the other stands directly in front of the charging beast, his chest right in between its long, curving horns. The bull's straining neck and forequarters are exaggerated, suggesting their immense strength. The bull itself arches as he powers forward, clearly excited by the affair. Light-headed in the heat, gazing at the bull-jumper framed by dizzying geometrics, I entered the Minotaur's world and began to hear his thoughts...

I smelled it even before the darkness shifted—a softening of the sour air, dampening the dusty floor ever so slightly, relaxing my nostrils, calming the fury that is my constant companion. Rain was coming. Queen Pasiphae was on her way, too. She occasionally visited me in secret, winding through the labyrinth in the dead of night, or sometimes during a storm. Always in the dark. Even she, who had borne and nurtured me, taught me to walk, raised me from infant calf to bull—even my mother was afraid of me now. I could smell her fear, arcing like lightning in the air.

The problem was my lust for blood. Seven maidens, seven boys. Every year, ever since my adolescent hormones began their violent surge. At first I didn't care whether they were virgins, but that's what King Minos always sent, and that's what I came to expect. I can only imagine how the king felt about me, his grotesque son, with the body of a boy and the head and tail of a bull. My very name was a combination of his own—Minos—and Taurus, a reference to the bovine who was my biological father. I was a constant reminder of the queen's infidelity, of her maddening obsession with the majestic white bull. It infuriated the king. For a while he turned to other women, but the queen was a powerful sorceress, and cast a spell on Minos so he was doomed to ejaculate centipedes, scorpions and serpents whenever he lay with a concubine. Not surprisingly, the situation proved fatal to his favorite mistresses.

To be fair, the queen—I was never allowed to call her "Mother," never allowed to have a mother, really—was not solely at fault. The king had owed a debt to the gods, and his queen was made to pay the price. A victim of divinely inflicted desire, she fell hopelessly in love with the handsome white bull, was overcome with passion, and became pregnant with what turned out to be me. The entire affair doubtless made the king feel brutish. Pasiphae nourished me at her breast when I was young, which must have been embarrassment enough, but when I hit adolescence and developed a taste for human flesh, the king could no longer disguise his contempt; he banished me to the labyrinth.

It was a vast subterranean prison—so dark I went blind in its depths, so endlessly circuitous it induced constant nausea and despair, so utterly terrifying it was surely the gateway to hell. And it was my home.

"Mother?" I dared to call out for her. To call her "Mother." I felt so lonely.

Silence.

"Mother, where are you?"

I felt her breath nearby. Light, like a breeze. Cool,

compared to my own dank exhalations. Would she speak to me?

"Mother, how long must I live in this tortuous chamber?"

Finally Pasiphae spoke. "There is no answer," she said. "Seek it lovingly."

This epigram roused me from my reverie as the day's heat filled my lungs. It had not been hard to morph into the Minotaur. I'd had my share of black spells, of swift descent, of wandering blindly, unable to claw my way out of confusion and despair. I knew how the Minotaur felt: dead end after dead end, nowhere to turn, helpless to do anything but wait. Hoping the darkness would lift, by some unknown grace, and light would return.

With that thought I realized, startled, that I had discovered the labyrinth after all. It was not a hilltop cakewalk, well-trodden by seekers and tourists, nor a sacred space in the halls of a great cathedral. It was not the palace complex at Knossos, but rather my confusing psychological journey through it—the journey that led, finally, to my daydream of the Minotaur and his mother's wise counsel.

> "There is no answer. Seek it lovingly."
>
> —Socrates

My own mother had framed these very words, penned in her easy, rhythmic handwriting, and posted them as a prayer on the bookshelf above her desk. *Let go of the need for certainty. The opposite is not indecision; it's openness, curiosity, willingness to accept complexity.* My mother knew this. And just as the Minotaur's mother had saved him—or at least comforted him—in the face of his father's rejection, my own mother had posted these words as a comfort. They had emerged from my subconscious in the voice of another mother whose child was lost and lonely—and as a reminder of the infinite entanglement that is the labyrinth, and the wisdom of adopting its lesson of embracing paradox.

Metamorphosis in La Guácima

Butterflies become a talisman for the future

Brightly colored wings explode in the air around me like silent fireworks. Paper-thin sheets of iridescent blue, broader than my hand, float inches from my face. Black-and-yellow swallowtails and bright green malachites drift aimlessly in swirling currents of warm air, while half a dozen orange-and-black Isabellas punctuate the shadows. This airborne choreography could be a scene from *The Birds*, except that the wings belong to butterflies.

Motionless, I watch as they flit from one leafy plant to another. There aren't any flowers here in the deep shade, but the butterflies don't seem to be in search of nectar; they're fluttering, fighting the breeze, resting, chasing each other and mating. Maybe they're playing? I don't know much about a butterfly's life, but my guide, Vanessa, is about to give me an education.

I'm at a butterfly farm—or *mariposario*—on the outskirts of La Guácima, a friendly village in central Costa Rica. One of the world's leading suppliers of butterfly chrysalises for live exhibits, it's aptly named The Butterfly Farm. The bulk of the "farm" is a 7,500-square-foot greenhouse, open to the air but enclosed with wire mesh so the butterflies can't escape—and most predators can't get in. Narrow pathways wind through shaded jungle, interspersed with sunny patches of bright red, yellow, and orange flowering plants: cosmos, passionflower, heliconia, lantana. One path leads to a sheltered grove where a small waterfall splashes into a quiet pool; this is the spot the blue morphos prefer.

The town of La Guácima is enthusiastic about the farm: Its streets are lined with butterfly murals painted on the sides of buildings: butterflies with flowers, butterflies with chrysalises, butterflies with graceful women. Most of the murals are lively and charming, but one disturbs me. It stretches across a single-story gray wall, brightening the entire side of the building with gigantic butterflies of all colors. The gigantic trompe l'oeil beauties hang side-by-side from a long clothesline, delicately attached by their wingtips with brightly painted clothespins. Their colors drip off like water: teardrops of red, yellow, green, blue and orange falling from flightless wings. It's a reminder of the reality of farming: The butterflies are livestock ...or do they mean something more?

Vanessa will show me around the farm. In her early twenties, she's tall and lean, with high cheekbones and almond eyes. Her left thumbnail is painted with a little blue butterfly. White streaks adorn its wings, and nearly microscopic specks of silver glitter decorate its black body. Matching blue butterfly earrings dance in front of Vanessa's long dark hair.

She holds a giant owl butterfly, her manicured thumb and forefinger pressing gently against the outsides of its two upper wings, which are closed. Overall, it's a dull brown-and-gray creature with a wingspan of eight inches. But each of its two back wings has markings that look like a gigantic eye in its center—a round, black "pupil" inside a golden "iris" that darkens to orangey-brown at the outer edge.

"You see the 'eyes'?" Vanessa asks. "Those are to protect the butterfly from predators." The eyespots are on the underside of the wings, so they show up when the wings are folded or seen from below—mimicking the appearance of an owl and deterring potential predators when the butterfly is resting or feeding.

"What animals eat the butterflies?" I ask, leaning in to look more closely.

"Mostly lizards and small songbirds—the same things that are eaten by owls."

I soften my gaze for a moment and imagine that I am a small animal. The butterfly's "eyes" glare menacingly at me. When the wings flit just a little, I startle; for a second, it really does look like the "owl" is alive.

"You see it!" Vanessa laughs. She stoops, picks up a twig the size of a sewing needle and uses it to gently unroll the butterfly's coiled proboscis—its feeding tube.

"Doesn't that hurt it?" I ask, alarmed.

"No, not if you're careful." Out and out and out she rolls the proboscis. Fully extended, it's more than an inch long. The butterfly doesn't seem to mind. It doesn't even twitch. "This is actually two strands that fit together like a zipper to form a tube. Butterflies drink nectar and the juices of fermented fruits. Sometimes they even drink the blood, sweat or tears from other animals. The tips of their legs can taste the plant they're standing on."

Vanessa releases the butterfly and it flutters over to a feeding station, landing on a browning piece of overripe banana and extending its proboscis for a sip. "Owl butterflies are crepuscular; they're most active at dawn and dusk. During the day they hang out here at the juice bar, getting drunk."

The "juice bar" is a feeding station: a two-foot-square plywood tabletop, once painted kelly green but now so chipped and faded it seems like part of the landscape. Cups of light red fruit juice and slices of rotting banana sit on the plywood. The whole thing is covered with owl butterflies—a couple dozen of them—sipping and flapping together, eyespots fluttering. The effect is weird and a little creepy. I understand why it scares predators away.

"They're getting sauced at the bar all day!" I observe. "Is that why they fly so erratically—because they're drunk?"

"Maybe," Vanessa allows. "But the unpredictable flight patterns help protect them from predators."

I have always thought that odd flight should have earned them the moniker "flutterby" instead of butterfly, but it's probably not realistic to hope for a change from the Old English name at this late date.

"What do they do at dawn and dusk?"

"They're mating, or defending their territory. Sometimes they stay joined for hours when they're reproducing."

"So they drink all day, and fight or philander in the evening —what thugs!"

We laugh and move down the path a few yards. Vanessa stops at one of the many banana trees, pulling a leaf down for us to view. Next to her thumbnail are three tiny spheres, each the diameter of a pinhead. "Here are some owl butterfly eggs that were laid recently," she says. I'm amazed she found these tiny eggs in such a huge space; she must know every inch of the place.

"These eggs will darken, but they won't get any bigger before the caterpillars emerge," Vanessa says. "The caterpillar's own eggshell is its first meal."

Hmmm. That's also a little weird and creepy.

She moves on to another banana plant and pulls down a long green leaf. Along its central spine are seven small caterpillars, each the same light-green color and smooth texture as the spine. The smallest ones are about a quarter of an inch long; the larger ones are close to an inch. "Newly hatched caterpillars are preyed on by lizards, frogs, birds, monkeys and snakes. Even the ants eat them," Vanessa says. "These are camouflaged with brown splotches that look like damaged leaves. Predators tend to overlook them."

Next she points out another batch of caterpillars. Six inches long, these are the same species, but look nothing like the little wigglers we just saw. They've changed from small, green and smooth to big, brown and hairy—and they've grown spiny horns on their backs and weird projections on their heads that make them look like tiny triceratops dinosaurs. "See how they're camouflaged to look like the bark of a tree? They'll stay in the caterpillar stage for two months, eating their host plant and growing quickly. They prefer plantains and bananas; farmers consider them a pest, unfortunately."

The Butterfly Farm—the first in Latin America—was founded in 1984 by an American Peace Corps volunteer named Joris Brinckerhoff and his wife, Maria Sabido. Brinckerhoff had degrees in economics and political science. At the time, he knew nothing about butterflies or entomology. But he'd had a chance encounter with a butterfly enthusiast and was also inspired by E. F. Schumacher's book, *Small is Beautiful*. Butterfly farming, Brinckerhoff thought, would be a good way for local families to generate income without causing ecological damage.

Over the years Joris and Maria learned a lot: to identify butterflies; to understand their various lifecycles, habitat and food requirements; to create breeding methodologies; and to collect and ship pupae so the butterflies had the best chance of survival. They learned how the weather affects butterfly reproduction: too little rain means the butterflies won't lay eggs; too much rain and the eggs won't survive. They also learned the ins and outs of government and airline regulations—shipping chrysalises can be complicated.

These days, the business is thriving. It's even been

used as a case study for Harvard MBA candidates. The farm is one of the leading suppliers of butterflies for live exhibits, exporting 400,000 chrysalises a year to 120 clients worldwide, including the Smithsonian. But they aren't all raised here. At a price of $1.60 to $2.40 per chrysalis—depending on supply and demand—the mariposario brings in enough income to significantly help families who raise butterflies and gather chrysalises on their own land. The income from these activities has lifted hundreds of Costa Ricans from poverty to the middle class.

After we've walked through the greenhouse garden, Vanessa shows me the pupae room, where hundreds of chrysalises are quietly working their magic, dissolving completely, then reorganizing their cells to transform from caterpillars into butterflies. Some are inconspicuous, and would be almost impossible to find in the wild: The band-celled sister (*Adelpha fessonia*), which will become a black butterfly with dramatic white stripes across its wings, looks like a shriveled brown leaf at this stage, as do the giant owl and many other species.

Some are showier. The familiar orange-and-black monarch (*Danaus plexippus*) completes its metamorphosis inside a pale aqua capsule encircled by a glinting golden ring. And the entire chrysalis of the orange-spotted tiger clearwing (*Mechanitis polymnia*) gleams in stunning gold.

"What about these metallic chrysalises? Don't they attract predators?" I'm not just thinking of hungry animals; these jewelry-like pendants surely attract humans, too. They look like actual gold, and I wouldn't mind hanging one on a thin chain around my neck, except that it's a living being, even in this sealed and silent state.

"We don't really know what the evolutionary explanation is," Vanessa admits. "There's still a lot of research to be done."

Next, Vanessa leads me through the Gallery of Human Transformation—a conference room adorned with huge banners explaining, in both English and Spanish, the Butterfly Farm's philosophy about the metamorphosis of butterflies as a metaphor for the possibility of human transformation. The banners mention things like "supraconscious potentialities" and "eternal union with the Supreme," which, although they sound appealing, are not really what I'm looking for today.

"OK," Vanessa smiles. "The tour is over. Thanks for visiting; have a great day."

The tour may be over, but I cannot leave; I need to spend more time with the butterflies. The shady waterfall area—the place that's filled with blue morphos—is my favorite spot. It's at the far end of a quiet path, a private place for contemplation in the midst of kinetic splendor.

But even more than the butterflies, it's the chrysalises that captivate me. Unborn wonders, they remind me of the Great Work of ancient alchemists: *solve et coagula*. Dissolve and coagulate. This is the exact work I'm doing now in an alchemical class: Dissolving hardened positions—negative habits and states of mind—then reconstituting them into a purer form: increased awareness. Physical into spiritual, lead into gold. This transformational work has been important in many cultures across time; in ancient Greece, for example, "psyche" was the word for both *soul* and *butterfly*.

Finally, it's closing time. The sun is slanting, and I must leave the mariposario. It has filled me with existential questions: Does a caterpillar have an inkling of what it will become? Does a butterfly remember its caterpillar days? What about my own future self—is it possible to even imagine?

As I walk back to central La Guácima I notice a mural I hadn't seen before. It depicts butterflies floating through space on ethereal wisps that remind me of the Butterfly Effect hypothesis: the idea that a small change in one place—like the flapping of one butterfly's wings—can lead to big changes in another place or time. An overwhelming sense of awe and gratitude arises in my heart. The butterflies and their chrysalises are talismans of possibility, reminding me how unknowable the future is and inspiring me to live my best life, right now.

Discussion Questions

1. In "Okonomiyaki," the author finds her husband's outgoing personality both admirable and embarrassing. Which of your own personality traits have both positive and negative aspects?

2. What food are you passionate about? Can you put its texture, flavor, and aroma into words? What associations does it bring up—family history, religious tradition, your childhood, a holiday or a time of year? How does it make you feel?

3. Do you have a favorite spot for watching wildlife? What have you seen? Have you ever felt connected to the divine through nature?

4. Is there any sense in which you are domesticated? What do we gain and lose when we sublimate our wildness?

5. Do you believe we're put on Earth for a preordained reason? Do you believe in free will? Are the two beliefs compatible?

6. What ancestral "stock" do you come from? What does that say about you?

7. How should America handle its Confederate monuments?
8. Think of a time when you "crossed the line." What did you take away from the experience?
9. How far into the future can you imagine? What would you do differently if you felt more connected to future generations? What if you felt more connected to your own future self?
10. The author identified with "my" red coquette. What places, political party, religion, sports teams, etc. do you consider "yours"? What are the pros and cons of that kind of identification?

If you enjoyed these stories

you might also like the ones in *Your Crocodile has Arrived: More true stories from a curious traveler.* It's an award-winning collection of stories that will have you:

- Journeying through Sri Lanka to see a 2,500-year-old tooth.
- Talking with a SETI scientist about flying saucers.
- Receiving a full-body chocolate massage.
- Seeing the world's largest earthworms—they grow to be 20 feet long!

The *Midwest Book Review* called it "a thoroughly engrossing read."

Readers' Favorite Awards gave it 5 stars, saying the "honest and brave" stories "weave adventure, humor and wisdom."

Other readers have called it wry, marvelously entertaining, evocative, quirky, profoundly moving, lively, gutsy, bold, thoughtful, warm-hearted, tender, engrossing, original and insightful.

ALSO, CHECK OUT

Lost, Kidnapped, Eaten Alive!
True stories from a curious traveler.
It's full of award-winning stories about adventures like:

- Accidentally marrying a Maasai warrior.
- Being eaten alive by leeches.
- Studying French kissing in Paris.
- Tracking down the Balinese healer who befriended Elizabeth Gilbert in her bestselling book *Eat, Pray, Love.*

Publisher's Weekly said the book is "part cultural tour, part prayer to the natural world ... circles the globe with lively adventures and intimate insights."

Kirkus Reviews called it "an engaging, meticulously observed journey that brings other cultures alive." Other readers have called it witty, intelligent, savvy, quirky, fresh and fun.

To get you started, here's the chapter—OK *most* of the chapter—about being kidnapped ...

A Sneak Peek from

Lost, Kidnapped, Eaten Alive!

True stories from a curious traveler

At a Crossroads

SOMEWHERE IN TUNISIA

I didn't know whether I was being kidnapped or rescued—that was what made my one big decision so difficult. That and the fact that I was young and foolish, and more than a little anxious about being stranded in the North African desert.

It all began quite innocently. Our bus had deposited Alan, my affable traveling companion, and myself at the door of a small, clean hotel in a dusty Tunisian village. The buildings were two stories high at most, covered with plaster, and whitewashed against the powdery red dust that enveloped the town and seemed to stretch forever. In the desperate heat of late afternoon, the place appeared to be completely deserted. Not a single shop was open and the dirt streets were empty: no vehicles, no pedestrians, not even a stray dog.

Inside, the 1940s-era hotel was as empty as the street. There were no brochures advertising nearby attractions (I suspected there *were* no nearby attractions); there was no "We accept VISA, MasterCard, and American Express" sign. There was no bouquet of silk flowers, no table, no couch on which weary travelers could rest. A lone white straight-backed chair stood sentry on the floor of exquisitely patterned blue and red ceramic tiles. The reception desk held a silver tray filled with mints.

I had only just met Alan, a wandering college student like myself, that morning. But I quickly decided he'd be great to travel with: he seemed friendly, calm and reasonable—not the type to freak out if a bus schedule changed or a train was delayed. Plus he spoke a little French, which I did not. Alan had a quick, cryptic conversation with the hotel clerk, and then translated for me. The clerk had pointed out that there were no taxis in the small town, and suggested that Alan hitch a ride to the local bar/restaurant—six miles out of town—for a beer and a bite to eat. It didn't occur to either of us that a woman shouldn't also venture out, and I was eager to see some sights, meet the locals, and have dinner. Of course I went along.

In retrospect, I realize I should have known better. We were in Tunisia, a country where women stay indoors and cover up like caterpillars in cocoons. The guidebooks had warned me to cover my shoulders and legs, and I felt quite modest and accommodating in a button-up shirt and baggy jeans.

When we arrived, I found that the place was more bar than restaurant, and that I was the only female present. Even the waiters were all men. But these details didn't seem important. After all, I had dressed conservatively, and decided to take the precaution—again, recommended by my guidebook—of avoiding direct eye contact with men. What could possibly go wrong?

Since I spoke neither French nor Arabic—and was assiduously avoiding eye contact—it was quite impossible for me to converse with anyone but Alan, who was busy putting his first-year college language skills to dubious use. I was bored. This was a plain-as-bread sort of establishment; there was no big screen TV soccer game, no video arcade, not even a friendly game of cards or a lively bar fight for me to watch. Just a lot of dark men in white robes, sitting in mismatched wooden chairs, speaking softly in a language I could not understand and drinking tiny cups of strong coffee. The bitter, familiar aroma was a meager comfort.

Then the music began; it sounded off-key and was startlingly loud and foreign—a little frightening, even. Next the belly dancers appeared: twelve gorgeous women, one after another, with long, dark hair, burnished skin, flowing diaphanous skirts in brilliant vermillion and aqua and emerald, gold necklaces, belts, bracelets, anklets. Gold everywhere: tangled cords jangling against long brown necks; fine, weightless strands decorating the swirling fabrics; heavy gold chains slapping in a satisfying way against ample abdominal flesh. They were a remarkable contrast to the stark room and simple furnishings, and I began to realize that things in Tunisia were not entirely as they first appeared.

The music quickened, and the dancers floated across the bar—which had somehow been converted into a stage—and around the room, weaving in and out among tables, lingering occasionally for a long glance at a pleased patron. Soon they were at our table, looking not at Alan but at me, urging me, with their universal body language, to join them.

Did I dare? My stomach clenched momentarily. I knew my dancing would be clumsy and ugly next to theirs, my short-cropped hair and lack of makeup un-attractively boyish, my clothing shapeless and without style or significant color. I wore no jewelry—as the guidebook suggested—just my glasses, which were not particularly flattering that year.

Of course I am relatively unattractive and clumsy in this foreign environment, I thought, *but there is no need to be priggish as well.* And the women were by now insistent, actually taking me by both hands and pulling me up to dance with them. Flushed with embarrassment, I did my best to follow their swaying hips and graceful arm movements as we made our way around the room once again. Even with the aid of the two beers, I was not foolish enough to attempt to duplicate their astonishing abdominal undulations.

As soon as I thought these exotic, insistent beauties would allow it, I broke the line and resumed my place—plain, awkward, very white, and completely out of my element—next to Alan. Thereafter, it was excruciatingly embarrassing for me to watch the dancers, and Alan agreed to accompany me back to the hotel. He, too, had had enough excitement for the evening and was ready to retire, so he asked the bartender to call us a cab. A fellow bar patron overheard the conversation and was kind enough to offer us a lift. The man wore Western-style clothing, understood Alan's French, and seemed safe enough; we felt fortunate to have arranged the ride in spite of our limited linguistic abilities and the fact that the night was still young.

But that's when the evening turned ugly. Two well-dressed, middle-aged men left the bar immediately after we did. We saw them get into a black Mercedes, and we watched in the rear-view mirror as they trailed us, just our car and theirs, bumping along a sandy road in the empty desert. There were no buildings,

A Sneak Peek

streetlights or pedestrians, and we saw no other vehicles.

I looked out the window, enjoying the vast, black night sky and trying to ignore my growing sense of anxiety. When we came to an unmarked Y intersection, our driver, in a bizarrely ineffective attempt at deception, headed steadily towards the road on the right, then veered off at the last second to take the road on the left. Neither Alan nor I could remember which direction we'd come from hours earlier, when it was still light out and we were not under the spell of Tunisian music and belly dancers and beer. The strange feigning and last-second careening alarmed us both.

And it got worse. Immediately after the incident at the intersection, the men in the car behind us revved the engine, chased us down and ran us off the road and into a ditch. They stood in the road, shouting and gesticulating wildly outside our car. My hands went icy in the warm night air. Despite—or perhaps because of—an imposing language barrier, we had the impression that the men who ran our car off the road were attempting to rescue us.

But what, exactly, were they rescuing us from? Was our driver a sociopathic kidnapper bent on selling us into slavery? A rapist? A murderer? And why were our "rescuers" so insistent? Was it out of the goodness of their hearts, or did they, too, have some sinister motive? We had to make a choice. One car would probably take us safely to our hotel; the other might lead to a terrifying fate. But we had no idea which was which.

In this moment of crisis, we clenched hands and Alan looked at me—somewhat desperately, I thought—for a decision. I tried to assess his strength, and wondered whether he was a good fighter. (Probably not—he was a Yale man.) My stomach churned, but I forced myself to concentrate. We had only two options: We could remain in the long black limo, hope it could be extricated from the ditch, and hope our volunteer driver really was the kind and innocuous man he had appeared to be.

Or we could bolt from the car, scramble out of the ditch, and as quickly as possible, put our rescuers and their car between ourselves and the man who had so generously offered us a ride. The two men were still shouting, and began to pound and slap the driver's window. Even so, Alan leaned towards staying. After all, he reasoned, it was only one man, and there were two of us. Surely we could overpower him and escape if it proved necessary.

I wanted to bolt. Even though there were two men in the "rescue" car, as opposed to only one in our vehicle, I had become certain, in some wholly subjective way, that our man was crazy, and I'd heard that crazy people can be quite strong. Plus, our apparent rescuers, the men who had just run us off the road, warned Alan that we were with "*un homme méchant! mauvais!*"—a wicked man. But the deciding factor was that these two men had actually gone to the trouble of following us out of the bar, chasing us down, running our car off the road and into a dusty ditch, and were now expending a great deal of energy trying to convince us of something.

Surely that constellation of actions bespoke a serious purpose, such as rescuing two foolish young travelers from a lifetime of misery in the North African desert. The two men *must* be rescuers; kidnappers were not likely to go to so much trouble, or to risk scratching or even denting their shiny black late-model Mercedes in the process.

Alan was no help; I had to make a decision myself, and quickly. But what about the downside? In the middle of all the commotion—and with Alan sitting next to me looking more than a little uncertain—I realized that we had not yet fully considered the potential negative consequences of an incorrect choice. If we chose to stay, and it was the wrong choice, the man would undoubtedly drive us to some sort of central kidnapping headquarters—probably an impenetrable, fortress-like stone building with dark, echoing corridors, or perhaps a sweltering, waterless hovel cleverly hidden in remote, sand-swept dunes. In that case, he would have a knife, or a gun, or evil partners—or perhaps all of the above—and the fact that the two of us probably could have overpowered him would be moot. We would be goners.

On the other hand, if we bolted, and that was the wrong choice, we would be double-goners because the two men could also turn out to be kidnappers or murderers who could easily overpower us. Downsides being equally awful, we decided to go with our gut. Or guts. The problem was that Alan's gut said stay, and mine said bolt....

I hope you've enjoyed the beginning of "At a Crossroads." To find out whether or not I made it out alive, you can read the entire story—plus twenty-two others—in *Lost, Kidnapped, Eaten Alive! True stories from a curious traveler*, available from your favorite bookseller.

About the Ouroboros Image

In Ancient Greek, ouroboros means *tail-devouring*. I'm captivated by the image—a serpent swallowing its own tail, being created through its own destruction.

The symbol's meaning is nearly as varied as the many cultures that have embraced it over millennia, but there's a beautiful unity in what it represents: regeneration, reincarnation, immortality, the cycle of life and death, the harmony of opposites, the eternal unity of all things, perpetuity and infinity.

The image used here is after a woodcut in a 1760 book titled *Uraltes Chymisches Werck von Abraham Eleazar,* or the *Age Old Chemical Work of Abraham Eleazar.*

Publication Notes

Some of these essays, or versions of them, have been published elsewhere, and some have won awards:

"At the Foot of Uluru"won a 2021 Travelers' Tales Solas Award.

"Cuba: Full of Flavor"was first published in *Wandering in Cuba: Revolution and Beyond* (Wanderland Writers, 2018).

"Cuba Through the Looking Glass" was first published in *Wandering in Cuba: Revolution and Beyond* (Wanderland Writers, 2018).

"Dreaming the Minotaur" was first published in *Wandering in Greece: Athens, Islands and Antiquities* (Wanderland Writers, 2020). The story won a Travelers' Tales Solas Award in 2021.

A version of "The Great Bald Eagle Fly-In at Klamath Basin" was published in *Travel Features and Photos: California's National Parks, Monuments, Trails, Seashores and Historic Sites.* (Bay Area Travel Writers, 2015).

"My Extra-Virgin Experiment" was first published in *Wandering in Greece: Athens, Islands and Antiquities* (Wanderland Writers, 2020).

About the Author

Laurie McAndish King grew up in rural Iowa, studied pre-med, art, and philosophy at Cornell College, and has traveled in 40 countries. She observes with an eye for natural science, and writes with a philosopher's heart. Her award-winning travel essays and photography have appeared in many publications, including *Smithsonian* magazine, Travelers' Tales' *The Best Women's Travel Writing* and more than a dozen literary anthologies. Her writing won a Lowell Thomas gold award and her mobile app about the San Francisco Waterfront earned a 5-star rating on iTunes.

Laurie also wrote *An Erotic Alphabet* (for which she was dubbed "The Shel Silverstein of Erotica") and co-edited two volumes in the *Hot Flashes: Sexy little stories & poems* series. She is an avid photographer—one of her photos was displayed for six months at the Smithsonian—and enjoys gardening, taxidermy, and, on occasion, visiting the Uncanny Valley.

Connect at LaurieMcAndishKing.com.

Gratitude

I wrote the stories that took place in Cuba and Greece after participating in Wanderland Writers workshops in those countries, and am grateful to workshop leaders Joanna Biggar and Linda Watanabe McFerrin for their generous and expert assistance in shaping those stories. Linda edited all the stories in this book, bringing her sharp editorial eye, astonishing intuitive abilities, and wise counsel to the process of transforming ideas into stories, and stories into the coherent whole of a book. And Jim Shubin, The Book Alchemist — who also happens to be my husband—put this book together in a way I love. He also holds me together in a way I love.

Laura Dunn, author of *Nine for Hilary: A 2016 Union of American Ancestors*, kindly introduced me to my own ancestor, Stephen Hopkins—which got me thinking about the issues in "Mayflower Memories." My aunt, Carol Sovern, lived in Trinidad for many years and introduced me to both the Asa Wright Nature Center and the Great Pitch Lake—places she knew I would adore. My parents took me on an eye-opening trip to Zimbabwe, where I met the elephants Janet and Rastus, and began to think about the dark side of domestication. Suzie Rodriguez was my partner in crime on the San Francisco waterfront; seeing it through her eyes gave me a richer appreciation of this endlessly fascinating city. And Lisa Alpine kept me writing when I felt like quitting; without her friendship and storytelling support the ideas in this book would never have made it onto the page. I am supremely grateful for all their assistance!

Made in the USA
Columbia, SC
05 February 2022

54861624R00159